Praise for *Cracking the Parenting Code*

"*Cracking the Parenting Code* is a fresh look into the mystery of parenting. Laura Heinsohn has done a thorough job researching the truth behind relationships with our children. This book will motivate you to examine and investigate the clues to the heart of your child. Straightforward and bold."
—**Peggy Roloff**, Huny on *Little People, Big World,*
TLC reality show

"Laura Heinsohn writes with compassion and wisdom about things all parents fear. She brings a fresh voice and original solutions to parenting issues. I'm adding this excellent book to my collection."
—**Rick Johnson**, author, *That's My Son* and *The Man Whisperer*

"*Cracking the Parenting Code* is creative and engaging, inspiring thought and encouraging action."
—**Joanne Zylstra**, vice-president of international operations, Childcare Worldwide

"Laura's 'insight through experience' is invaluable to this incredible resource. Honest and transparent, she is not only sharing what she's learned through interviews and coaching, but through life lessons. This book can bring healing to parents and healthy parenting to children."
—**Tammy Dunahoo**, national director of Foursquare Women, Arkansas district supervisor, The Foursquare Church

"Bravo for *Cracking the Parenting Code*! There is nothing more precious than really knowing the hearts of your children. This book is a delight and a breath of fresh air in helping me discover the path to building lasting relationships. I have started to implement some of these principles, and they are life changing. Follow the clues and you'll be on your way."
—**Jennifer Evans**, wife, mother, pastor's wife, business consultant executive, retreat speaker

CRACKING THE PARENTING CODE

6 CLUES TO SOLVING THE MYSTERY OF MEETING YOUR CHILD'S NEEDS

LAURA LEE HEINSOHN

NEW HOPE
PUBLISHERS
Birmingham, Alabama

New Hope® Publishers
P. O. Box 12065
Birmingham, AL 35202-2065
www.newhopepublishers.com

New Hope Publishers is a division of WMU®.

Library of Congress Cataloging-in-Publication Data

Heinsohn, Laura Lee, 1957-
   Cracking the parenting code : 6 clues to solving the mystery of meeting your child's needs / Laura Lee Heinsohn.
      p. cm.
   ISBN 978-1-59669-207-7 (sc)
   1. Parenting--Religious aspects--Christianity. 2. Child rearing--Religious aspects--Christianity. I. Title.
   BV4529.H44 2008
   248.8'45--dc22
                        2008037251

- The quotes from Charles de Gaulle on page 114 and from Abraham Joshua Heschel on page 37 were taken from *Random House Webster's Quotationary* by Leonard Roy Frank.
- "Shadows" lyrics by Karen Peris, Don Peris, Amy Grant (p. 174).
- "Kids' Clues" from Billy on page 83 was cited by Mary Southerland in her article, "Unleashing the Power of God in My Life-Discipline (part 5)"; Pastors.com/Ministry Toolbox, Issue #194-Home; http://legacy.pastors.com/RWMT/article.asp?ID=194&ArtID=7975

ISBN-10: 1-59669-207-3
ISBN-13: 978-1-59669-207-7

N084133 • 0109 • 4M1

For my mommy,
Dorene Lydia
A woman of dignity and perseverance

Contents

Foreword

Not long after my first child was born, I realized there was a gap in parenting literature. I had every book imaginable about what to feed my daughter, what to teach her, and what stages of development I should be seeing. What I didn't find in the literature was any discussion about what was happening to me! This little baby challenged everything I knew and thought I knew about myself. *Who was I and who was I becoming?* Not only was I supposed to figure out what she needed and who she was becoming, I had to figure out what I needed and who I was becoming. On top of that challenge, I had to figure out who my young husband was as a father and how we would do this together! Looking back—what a daunting task was set before us.

Today, 30 years later, I face another challenge, similar but even more daunting in some ways. I am the children's clinical director for my community's behavioral health center. There are 1,200 families enrolled in our programs. What do I see and hear? Kids are hurt and lost and left behind every day. Many of them will be wounded for a lifetime. But I am also encouraged as I see families, moms and dads, grandparents and foster parents, who are desperately trying to make their families work.

Now those parents have another resource to help them in their efforts, a book I am thankful fills the gap I noticed so many years ago: *Cracking the Parenting Code*. Laura Heinsohn and I met about three years ago. When she started talking about her work and her ideas I immediately got excited. She was talking about things I had always thought about and tried to teach parents. Laura didn't talk about skills training or parent education. Laura challenged herself and others to really investigate their lives and hearts. Her work challenges all of us to look at our past and our family of origin and discover what we learned, how we were hurt, and how we were nurtured.

Our job is not to identify someone to blame for whatever is going wrong in our lives or in our children's lives. Our job is to search our own mind, soul, and spirit right now and to be honest about ourselves and to teach our children to do the same. With this process at work, we can then attempt to develop healthy, wonderful relationships with our spouses and children. The greatest gift I have as a parent is the friendship I have found in my adult children and their willingness to include me in their families.

What do children need? Food, clothing, shelter, education, and rules? These items are not necessarily on Laura's list. What is on her list? Children need to feel safe and trust their parents, to be valued, and to be understood; and then they need to have a purpose, support, and boundaries. Sounds simple. I think what Laura is calling us to do is to be present to our children, who are changing every day. She is calling us to push down our fear, pain, expectations, and myths so that we can really meet the needs of the person in front of us who calls us Mom or Dad.

Laura has invested her heart, soul, and mind in this project. She has trusted her Lord to lead her where He has called. She is called to deliver this message and if you are holding this book, you are called to hear it and respond. I wish you courage and wisdom on your journey.

Paula Lupo, MA, LPC
Children's Clinical Director
Mohave Mental Health Clinic, Inc.
Lake Havasu City, Arizona

Hope for Families

When children emotionally, physically, or spiritually walk away from their parents' love, values, convictions, and beliefs, it leaves parents bewildered, distraught, and often angry. I know, because I was one of those parents. During the time my daughter and I were estranged I was inundated with two thoughts: *What did I do wrong? What could I have done differently?* I know this is not unusual. Over the last few years I have talked with hundreds of parents who are grappling with these same questions.

As I wrote this book and in the months following, two close friends and a relative lost their precious children to senseless deaths. I dedicate this book to those courageous parents.

My husband's cousin, Shane Matthews, was extremely bright. He had rich brown eyes, soft dark hair, and a beautiful timid smile. Tragically, he dropped dead while vacuuming the floor of a church where he was learning to live an alcohol-free life and await God's direction. He was born January 11, 1980. He'd abused his body so terribly that it stopped functioning. He didn't know he was born with a predisposition to alcoholism. Shane was born into a family with two incredibly loving parents and a rich, four-generation Christian heritage.

My sweet friends Tom and Laura also lost their son tragically. One morning I was attending a home-group meeting—Laura and Tom were seated next to me. During the lunch break, Tom went home and found his son Tyler had shot himself, outside on their property. Tom and Laura have ministered the love of God their entire marriage and were devastated by the loss of their only son.

Yesterday, I received a phone call from my son who told me that a friend's daughter was found dead, as the result of a self-imposed alcohol-related accident. She was barely 21.

Each one of these parents—while raising their children—believed their children would grow up to change the world. They loved their children deeply, wanted nothing but the very best for them, and provided every opportunity for them to succeed. Now these devoted, adoring parents are trying to survive in a world in which their children exist only in their memories. They go to bed at night haunted by the same questions I've struggled with: *What did I do wrong? What could I have done differently?*

Maybe you're a first-time parent who feels insecure and unqualified, and you don't want your child to someday walk away from your beliefs and convictions. Maybe you're a parent who didn't realize having a child would awaken so many unfamiliar emotions, and you want to avoid the mistakes of those who have gone before you. Perhaps you're an exhausted single parent in need of hope and encouragement. Or maybe you're a stepparent or foster parent needing deeper insight and creative ways to connect with your children, blending your family. Maybe you're a struggling parent whose teen has shut you out of her life, and you're searching for ways to reconnect. Maybe you're a perplexed parent of adult children who are currently estranged from you.

No matter what place you are in your relationship with your children, this book is intended to help you:

- Gain hope and encouragement as you discover the six clever clues to connect or reconnect with the hearts of your children, increasing the odds that they will embrace your values, lifestyle, and convictions.

- Learn to look at how you were parented—what worked and what didn't—bringing resolution to your past and breaking negative cycles.

- Consider how you are parenting, identifying, and resolving physical, emotional or spiritual struggles.

- Learn to see your children differently, gaining deeper insight into their individual needs.

- Discover issues and concerns that your children have that many parents may not think about.

I wrote this book because I am genuinely concerned about what is—oftentimes unknowingly—happening in our families. We want our children to change the world, but instead the world is changing them. This book is my way of saying: "It doesn't have to be that way." If one question, one suggestion, or one story in this book spares you the deep anguish of watching your child walk away from you—if what I share makes even one day or one hour with your child richer—then my mission is accomplished and this book has done its job!

Is There Hope?
Recently I read the true story of a man who struggled with his son's "meth" (methamphetamine) addiction. Throughout his book he uses his intellect to try to understand and help his son. I was deeply touched by his desperation and anguish, but the deeper tragedy is

that his only hope is to rely on human beings and his own mind. How sad. To believe you can think your way out of something is dumbfounding to me. Maybe it's because I'm not that smart.

I know that throughout my parenting journey I would have been lost without the incredible love, direction, and wisdom of the Holy Spirit. He was there to hold my hand when my hand was limp. He was there to mend my heart when my heart was broken. He was there to calm my mind when my mind was tormented. He comforted me when I couldn't lift my head up off the pillow.

If you are following Jesus, the Holy Spirit is there for you too, no matter where you are in this parenting puzzle. So as you journey through the pages of this book looking for clues to your children's heart, please know that you need not walk alone. You can have God with you—you need only to call on Him. Yes, there is hope.

And because I believe it is so important to know this hope in Jesus I would like to share with you now the story of how He changed me.

The Life for Me

When I was young, I wanted to believe in God. My one continual prayer was that my daddy would quit drinking. At a very young age, I observed his normally clear words turn sloppy; his kind eyes turn crazy; and his lighthearted step turn to a sloppy stagger. Unfortunately, as I grew, my father's alcoholism grew. My thought pattern became: *If God were real and He loved me, He would make my daddy quit drinking.* Day by day, month by month, year by year, my one and only prayer seemed to be ignored, so I reasoned God was in the same category as Santa Claus. By the time I was a preteen any traces of faith had disappeared.

Soon I began drinking and using drugs. At 16, I discovered I was pregnant the same day my mom told me she was divorcing my dad. I never told my parents I was pregnant and secretly had an abortion two weeks later—to this day it is the biggest regret of my life. At 18, I was responsible for a drunk-driving accident that nearly took my life. At 20, I moved to Australia to live with a man I'd only known three days. After six weeks, confused and tired, I headed back to the United States.

Within two days I found a two-week temporary job as the secretary for a man named Rick, who believed God was real. I asked him question after question about his religion, and he patiently answered each one.

As the days went on, our spiritual discussions became more intense, and I confided to him my deep-rooted disappointment with God. "If God is real how come He didn't answer my one and only prayer when I was a child?"

"Lori [my nickname], you and your dad both have free will," he calmly explained. "God can't make you do something you are unwilling to do. Your dad made the choice to continue to drink, and his daily choices are taking from him the incredible life God intended him to have. God sees his struggles, just as He is with you. God heard your prayers. He probably intervened many times, but your dad didn't heed the call. It is your father's choice not to spend his life with God."

I rubbed my head.

"Jesus died for you on a cross a long time ago, for your sins. He desires to have a relationship with you."

The magnitude of what my boss was saying hit me like ice-cold water thrown in my face. *Uh, oh. If God is really real, then I am in big trouble. I've made such a horrible mess of my life. If I tell Rick what I did he'll probably agree I'm beyond forgiveness.* I got brave.

"OK, Rick, if God is real and Jesus really died for me— just me—then I'm in really big trouble. I've done some terrible, terrible things in my life, and I don't think God could forgive me." I went on to describe every awful thing I had done in my life and looked intently into his eyes to see if he'd react. Rick's eyes remained so kind and warm; he never flinched.

"Lori, one sin isn't worse than another. God loves you, and He forgives you. You only have to ask. See this stool right here," He pointed to the office stool. "It's like your entire life you've been standing on that stool making decisions. You're the boss and nobody is going to tell you what to do or how to live. Life is all about you."

What he was saying really struck home. It reminded me of what my sisters had been telling me all of my life. They ran around the house singing, "Whatever Lori wants, Lori gets," which infuriated me.

He went on, "Am I right?" I nodded in agreement. "Now, you're balancing on the stool, looking at your life, thinking you've made some really stupid choices. You can get off the stool, and let God help you make decisions and show you how to live. And you can give Him charge of your life, which in my opinion is more secure and safe. Or you can continue your balancing act and live by your own rules."

"How do I know what He wants me to do when I have no idea where to start?"

"A great place to start is by reading your Bible, finding good friends who are living their lives for God, and finding a great place to worship and learn about God," he said.

I was perplexed; I only knew one Jesus freak, as I used to refer to them, and she seemed like a fruitcake.

Turning Point

The next weekend was my 21st birthday. Several friends and family congregated at a local bar. I was seated on a bar stool at the counter next to my father, "Lori, I'm so blankity-blank (he had a colorful vocabulary) proud of you for turning 21. Now you can go out and drink with me anytime you want."

I felt nauseated. *Yuck! Had my life really come to this? I'm sitting on a bar stool next to my father. Am I going to turn out just like him?* I could hear Rick's voice ringing in my ear, "You can choose to live your life standing on the stool, being the boss of your life, or you can step off and turn control over to One who is wiser." I picked up my rum and Coke and it tasted dreadful. I looked around the room. The dark atmosphere seemed creepy, the music dark and depressing, the smell of the musty, beer-stained carpet repulsive. *If I choose to live on this bar stool the rest of my life, I will end up like my father—tormented by shame, guilt, and regret.* I walked out of the bar that night knowing what I needed to do.

I went home and prayed a simple prayer: "God, I've made such a mess of my life. Please forgive all the awful things I've done. I want to live for You, and I need You to show me how. I desire to live the life You have for me."

That decision was the greatest decision of my life. Spiritually, I leapt off the bar stool from which I had been running my life and took my place on solid ground. I gave control over to Jesus, and I felt safe, secure, and loved.

I decided I'd try this "new way." I remember the first time I read 1 Corinthians 13:4, the passage about love. I was amazed that something that beautiful was in the Bible. I never knew. What else had I been missing? I had previously thought the Bible was filled with hellfire and damnation. I began telling everyone I knew about that Scripture. *Love is patient, love is kind.* I became a little obnoxious.

Three months after I accepted Jesus, I met my husband, Randy, at a friend's party. Everyone told me to stay away from him, because he was from a religious family. They told him to stay away from me, because I was a troubled party girl. We fell in love and were married three months later. Sixteen months after that, we had our first child. We found a great church full of young families, made great friends, and grew to know God in a very personal, sweet way. I have experienced what Ephesians 3:20 says, *"Now to him who is able to do immeasurably more than all we ask or imagine, according to his power that is at work within us"* (NIV).

I have lived a life that I could have never even imagined. I've experienced an unconditional love so deep and pure, joy inexpressible; I've been to places I'd always dreamed of; and I've been honored to minister Christ's love, grace, joy, and hope to children and families around the world. Did I get lucky? No, I just accepted the call when, in a pretty dark hour, sitting at a bar, Christ reached out to me.

If you've read the story of my life and want to stop running your own life, ask yourself these investigative questions: Do you believe God is real? Do you desire a richer, fuller life? Do you believe Jesus, God's Son, died for *you,* to forgive *your* failures and wrong choices? Do you believe Jesus rose from the dead and is alive today, ready to give you new life? Do you want to be free from guilt and shame? Do you want God to be the director of your life?

If you answered yes to these questions then I think you're ready—like I was—to jump down off the stool of control and put God where He belongs! If the things of this world are leaving a bad taste in your mouth, then come, *"taste and see that the LORD is good"* (Psalm 34:8 NIV). Pray the following prayer silently or out loud:

Heavenly Father,
Please forgive me for all the wrong things I've done in my life. I desire to put You where You belong, in control of my life. Please come into my life. I need You to guide me through the next few minutes, hours, days, weeks, and years, to show me the way of peace. Please help me find a community of godly people who strive to live for You and can be living examples as how to navigate my new life. Help me when I read Your Word (the Bible), make it clear to me so I can understand it. I love You! Amen.

Author's Note:
The stories and cases you read about in this book are true, however, some names, family structures, and locations have been changed to protect the privacy and identity of the families who bravely and courageously let me into their lives.

In each chapter, you will find some or all of the following elements:

FBI Questions—thought-provoking questions that will help you understand your upbringing, your children, and yourself. Sometimes general; sometimes divided into two categories as below.

- *Uncovering Clues in Your Childhood*—questions to help you discover how your upbringing affects the ways you now parent.

- *Uncovering Clues in How You Parent*—questions to help you discover what you are doing well and what you are doing poorly with your children, identifying the struggle.

Cracking the Code—creative solutions to connect with your children.

From the Heart of an Investigator—insights from the author's heart and personal experiences.

Kid's Clue—just a few funny sayings from children to make you laugh between chapters.

PART ONE:

THE MYSTERY

Mystery: something hidden requiring special revelation.... In biblical Greek it is truth revealed
—Spirit-Filled Life Bible

I SPY:

The Accidental Making of a Private Parenting Investigator

So Moses sent them to spy out the land of Canaan, and said to them, "Go up this way into the South, and go up to the mountains."
—Numbers 13:17

We must learn from our mistakes, a process that can begin once we acknowledge them. And we must vow not to repeat them. And especially an investigator should not develop tunnel vision on a specific case. Instead, he or she should always keep an open mind and let only the evidence lead to the case's solution.
—Dr. Henry C. Lee (forensic investigator) with Thomas W. O'Neil, *Cracking More Cases*

I became a private parenting investigator by accident. Let's just say it kind of fell into my lap.

One day I was minding my own business, sitting on the sofa, eating potato chips, when I turned on the television. I couldn't believe what was happening right before my eyes, the beautiful young woman in the long black gown wasn't just anyone—it was Katie Harman. As a little girl, Katie had been a member of The Bee-Bop Kids, a performing arts team I had directed. Her mother and I are good friends. I blinked once, twice. Was this real? Was this truly the Miss America pageant? We had just moved from Oregon to Arizona and I knew Katie had entered the Miss Oregon contest, but I didn't know she won. Now I sat watching the TV screen for the next two hours, mesmerized as the contestants were whittled down to the top ten.

Tears fell from my eyes as Katie belted out an operatic aria and dramatically fell to her knees. She made it into the top five. I began to shake as she stood holding hands with one last fellow contestant. And then came the announcement: "The new 2002 Miss America is…"—my hands sweating, my heart thumping wildly—"Miss Oregon, Katie Harman." I shot off the couch, leapt in the air, and started jumping up and down.

"Randy, oh my goodness, oh my goodness," I shouted to my husband. "Katie got Miss America! Katie got Miss America! I don't believe it! Oh my goodness!" I ran around the living room like I was dancing with bees. My husband laughed at me as I kept shrieking over and over "I don't believe it, I don't believe it." As I glanced up at the television, I saw my friend Darla and her husband Glen with mouths gaping open and stunned looks on their faces.

With a new sense of patriotism I sobbed as Katie was crowned Miss America. As she walked down the runway to "Here She Comes, Miss America," I couldn't help but say a little prayer for her.

"Dear God, please keep your hand on this little American angel. Watch over her steps and guard her life." After all, this was my friend Darla's baby girl. It was the least I could do.

Same Prayer, Different Story

I found myself saying the same prayer again a few days later when another friend called to tell me about her son, Jack.

"Lori," a quiet voice whispered.

"Yes, this is Lori, who is this?" I replied curiously, not recognizing the shaky voice on the other end of the line.

"This is Julie," she said softly. She sounded like she was choking back tears.

"Are you OK? What's the matter?" I asked anxiously. After a long pause, Julie began to cry.

"It's Jack," her cries broke into sobs. "Jack's been arrested again."

I sat stunned. *What should I say? What could I say that would help?* Jack was her son. He had grown up with my son, Nicholas, in the same circle of friends; we had become like family. I listened to the anguish and heartbreak in her voice. As she described the heart-wrenching path her son had chosen, we both wept. Forty-five minutes later we said our good-byes, and I repeated the prayer I had prayed for Katie just a few days earlier. "Dear God, please keep your hand on Jack. Watch over his steps and guard his life."

Again I thought to myself: *How can this be? We raised our children together; we had the same philosophies, morals, the same God. Why then did one child become Miss America while another went to jail?*

Over the next few weeks I was tormented by confusion. Katie had the world in the palm of her hand while Jack was being kept from the world in jail. It didn't make sense to me. Both children were raised in stable, middle-class, two-parent homes where Mom stayed home and Dad went to work and the family attended church together. Yet the two children couldn't have turned out more differently. I was baffled. Two questions kept nagging at me: Why did these children turn out so differently? What happened in their seemingly parallel lives that caused them to choose such different paths?

This truly was a mystery!

The Hunt for Answers

I knew I needed to get to the bottom of what is happening in our families, but how? How does an investigator solve a mystery?

To learn how they do it, I went straight to investigative sources: I picked the brain of undercover investigative expert Detective Sergeant Dean Hennessey, a longtime family friend, to discover how a detective thinks. I analyzed US Bureau of Justice statistics (criminal statistics) to find similarities in family structures. I pored through the work of renowned forensic scientist Henry C. Lee and the work of bounty hunter Joshua Armstrong. I also extensively researched the Federal Bureau of Investigation (FBI) and the Central Intelligence Agency (CIA), looking at how they solve problems. Their expertise helped me learn how to follow the leads and find the missing answers I needed to solve the baffling mystery of why children become estranged emotionally, spiritually, or physically from their loved ones.

I began my investigation like a real detective, by extensive questioning. I talked to friends whose children walked away from them physically, emotionally, or spiritually and documented their responses. One interview led to another and soon I was interviewing the children themselves, now grown. As the months rolled on, I found myself engaged in deep conversation with more than 1,000 strangers I met on airplanes, at the gym, in the grocery store, at baseball games, conferences, and many other places—people of different races, religions, and classes—from around the United States. I listened for hours to the heartaches and joys of parents, single parents, foster parents, and stepparents. I began to study the family structures of different cultures and traveled to Europe; there, onboard a cruise ship with people from around the world, I engaged people in intense conversations about how they were raised and how they raise their children. My goal: to understand why children walk away from their parents, whether physically, emotionally, and/or spiritually, and to discover how to prevent that from happening.

Throughout my three-year investigation, when interviewing someone, I would start the conversation with two questions: Are you living your life with the same values and convictions as those your parents raised you with? Are you raising your children the same way you were raised?

As a parent for more than 27 years and a parenting coach to several hundred parents over the past four years, I assumed I knew what people would say: "My parents were hypocrites, telling me not to smoke while smoking a cigarette, telling me I shouldn't use swear words then yelling and cursing at the driver who cut them off." Turns out I didn't know as much as I thought I did. I began documenting the responses and categorizing them. After documenting the first 200 persons in my investigation, I knew my assumptions were way off. An overwhelming majority—196 of the first 200—of the people I interviewed said they left their parents values and beliefs, because their <u>parents didn't respect each other and conveyed hostility to them about the other parent</u>. Only four stated that they embraced their parents' values and convictions and are raising their children in similar ways. It made me wonder how many other parenting assumptions I had that were wrong.

My "Aha!" Moment

When I shared with people my private parenting investigation, nearly everyone responded with intense curiosity and asked me the *same* million-dollar question, "What did you discover?" Soon I found myself speaking to small groups about these top-secret discoveries, which led to launching Family Bureau of Investigation (FBI) Parent Workshops teaching these life-changing principles.

The theme of this book and my "aha!" moment, as Oprah calls it, both came during a revelation I had while vacationing in Mexico. Nearly every person who walked away from their parents' lifestyle, convictions, or values kept saying the same thing: "I needed something from my parents that they couldn't or didn't give me. I wanted my parents to stop fighting—I needed to feel secure." "<u>I needed to be heard</u>." "I needed to feel my life had purpose." "I needed my mom or dad to support me, at least come to one game." "I needed to have more lenient boundaries." "I needed for someone to care."

This common truth kept rising to the surface: we connect and bond with those who meet our needs. If someone doesn't meet at least one of our needs, we bond with someone else who does. Our children are no different. They connect with those who meet their needs! If parents aren't meeting their needs, they will bond with friends and acquaintances that do. In my investigation, children who embraced their parents' lifestyle, values, and convictions had parents who met many of their needs. Children who walked away from their parents had parents who met very few of their needs.

The Six Clever Clues

I documented many, many needs, but the top six in my research were:

- Children need to feel safe and secure—to be with people they can trust.

- Children need to be valued and understand why they are valuable.

- Children need to be heard and understood.

- Children need to have purpose not pampering.

- Children need to have support.

- Children need boundaries—ones that are neither too strict nor too lenient.

Now that you know the top six needs, take a look at how you were raised and see if you discover any important revelations.

 FBI Questions:
Uncovering Clues in Your Childhood
1. Your parents, married or divorced, respected one another and rarely conveyed hostility to each other or argued in front of their children. ☒ YES ☐ NO

2. You felt that your parents listened to you. ☒ YES ❑ NO

3. You were given opportunities to serve others and developed a sense of purpose as a child. ☒ YES ❑ NO

4. You were raised with a healthy view of your worth— neither overvalued nor undervalued. You were taught that your true value was being a child of God. ☒ YES ❑ NO

5. You felt supported as a child. ☒ YES ❑ NO

6. The boundaries set for you as a child were consistent—not too strict or too lenient. ☒ YES ❑ NO

If you answered:

☒ yes to all six questions, you probably have a great relationship with your parents.

• yes to three to five of these questions, you probably have a fair to good relationship with your parents.

• yes to one to two questions, chances are you don't feel very closely connected to your parents.

• yes to zero questions, you possibly have a strained relationship with your parents, if any relationship at all.

Of the more than 1,000 people to whom I asked these questions, nearly every person who walked away from their parents answered no to all six questions. As children, these individuals did not develop a healthy trust for their parents because their parents were constantly arguing, they rarely felt heard, and they felt that both parents had inconsistent boundaries for them, which caused confusion. They also stated they never felt supported nor, as children, did they believe their lives had any special purpose.

As you continue through the book, these questions are intended to help you begin examining your childhood, so that the feelings and thoughts stirred up by the process will give you greater insight into what your own children are currently feeling and thinking.

FBI Questions:
Uncovering Clues in How You Parent

Now consider how each of your children would answer the following questions:

1. My parents, married or divorced, respect one another, and rarely convey hostility or argue in front of me. ❑ YES ❑ NO

2. I always feel heard. ❑ YES ❑ NO

3. I am given opportunities to serve others and develop a sense of purpose. ❑ YES ❑ NO

4. I am being raised with a healthy view of my worth—not overvalued or undervalued. I am being taught that my true value is being a child of God! ❑ YES ❑ NO

5. I feel I am being supported in the ways I need to be. ❑ YES ❑ NO

6. The boundaries set for me are consistent—not too strict, not too lenient ❑ YES ❑ NO

If your child would answer:

- yes to all six questions, you most likely have built a strong bond with your child.

- yes to four to five questions, you have some room for improvement.

- yes to two to three questions, then it's time to get to work doing some serious relationship building.

- yes to zero questions, you and your child could be heading for trouble. Take this book seriously and do the hard work!

It's important to note that each of our children have different needs. What one child needs from his/her parents, another child in the same family may not need or may need it in an different way.

How Do I Discover What My Children Need?

Your main investigative assignment in this book is to find out the needs of each of your children. But how to do that? Some needs may be obvious; some may be obscure. Some children are easy to read; others are a lot more difficult. Because each child has different needs, it's important to know each unique child! You are probably saying to yourself, "Of course I know my children. I'm their parent." But do you really? Do you know what their most embarrassing moment is? Do you know what their proudest moment is? Do you know what their greatest fear is? Do you know if you do anything that causes them embarrassment? Do you know their thoughts about how you treat their father or mother? Do you know their thoughts about how you treat them, and how their other parent treats them?

When we ask our children heartfelt questions, like we would ask a co-worker or friend, our children feel we are genuinely interested in them. When people ask you questions about your feelings and opinions, do you feel like they are genuinely interested in you? I do. However, if people never ask my opinion about anything, I assume they don't care about what I think or how I feel. Our children are no different. If we don't ask them timely questions and take the time to truly listen, they'll assume their opinions and feelings don't matter.

So get ready! Throughout this book you will be asking and answering lots of questions, thought-provoking questions, which, if answered honestly, will lead you to your child's specific individual needs.

But Before We Start...

It's important to understand that I am not a parenting professional, family therapist, psychologist, or counselor. I am a mother, grandmother, parenting coach, workshop leader, mentor, and a self-proclaimed private parenting investigator. I have mentored and coached hundreds of parents of young children and teens and parents of grown children, both nationally and internationally. More than 25 years of personal experience with my two children (now grown), seven grandchildren, and seven foreign exchange students, along with the wisdom I've gleaned from experts, including professional family counselor Paula Lupo, have given me valuable insight into the family. From 1989 to 1996 I also worked extensively with several hundred children as the founder and director of the international dance/drama evangelistic outreach team The Bee-Bop Kids. When push comes to shove, I consider myself a concerned mama who has experienced the heartbreak of a child walking away and who has uncovered some important information that parents need to know.

Halt! Before you start following the clues we've got some important matters to take care of.

- The purpose of *Cracking the Parenting Code* is to help you discover clever clues to your children's heart, not to evaluate if you are or are not a good parent. In her book *Mom, I Hate My Life!* Sharon A. Hersh writes, "The reality is that all of us, if observed over a long period of parenting, would come out looking both very good and very bad." We, as parents, are quick to brand ourselves as guilty of messing up our children—and perhaps we do—but we are also guilty of loving them deeply.

- Please understand that our children, like ourselves, are free to make their own choices. During my investigation I interviewed many incredibly loving parents who steered their children in the right direction and raised two or three children who embraced their convictions and values, yet had one or two others who wanted nothing to do with them. There are no guarantees; we are imperfect and we live in an imperfect world with imperfect spouses, children, friends, and family. Our only saving grace: a perfect God we can run to.

> Beyond all mystery is the mercy of God.
> —Abraham Joshua Heschel, *God in Search of Man*

- We won't be playing the blame game. The investigator's job is to *investigate* not *prosecute*. The reason we will look at the past is to better understand it, not to build a case against our parents. They did their best with the training and knowledge they'd been given.

- This is your *private* investigation. This about you and your perception of your childhood and your current parenting. This isn't about your husband or wife, ex-husband or ex-wife, and what they are doing right or wrong. We have no control over how others think or what others do. Try to keep focused on your life and your experiences as a child and with your children.

- You might find that through your investigation you will uncover distressing memories. I challenge you to stay the course, and to use the tools presented in this book to work through them. After all, the truth really will set us free.

- This book doesn't have all the answers—just as each child is different, the problems and solutions to parenting each child are different as well. It's not only your job as a parenting investigator to discover the missing pieces, but also to find solutions to meeting your child's specific needs. Don't panic. Many solutions will be provided in this book. However, proficient detectives and parents know, it's your job—when you uncover something beyond your capabilities to solve—to enlist the help of a professional or consult the many professional resources available.

For example, Rene and Michael came to one of my FBI Parent Workshops and discovered that their blended family was in shambles, because both Rene and Michael were raised with extremely different boundaries: hers lenient, his strict. Once the problem was exposed, they could do something about it. They learned more about boundaries through private counseling, books, and the Internet. Please, if you discover something you can't solve, don't hesitate to contact a professional. You will also find many resources listed in the back of this book and on my Web sites www.lauraleeheinsohn.com and www.fbiparent.com.

Now grab your magnifying glass, put on your Sherlock Holmes hat, we've got mysteries to solve!

Kid's Clue

"No one notices what I do until I don't do it."
—Lorrie, 14
from *Wit and Wisdom from the Peanut Butter Gang* compiled by H. Jackson Brown, Jr.

CHAPTER 2

Priority 1:

Searching for Truth,
the Whole Truth,
and Nothing but the Truth!

Surely you desire truth in the inner parts; you teach me wisdom in the inmost place.
—Psalm 51:6 (NIV)

The sole objective of any investigation must be and always must be, the search for "the truth."
—Dr. Henry C. Lee with Thomas W. O'Neil,
Cracking Cases

As detectives can tell you, when a person goes missing, there were often telltale signs that trouble was brewing, that something was amiss. A person who is planning to run away may have been giving out signals for months, sometimes years.

A well-trained detective can put together a clear picture of a family's dynamics in a matter of hours by asking significant as well as seemingly trivial questions, listening intently to the answers, discerning body language and speech patterns, backtracking, and interviewing family and friends. Often the detective can piece together a likely scenario of reasons the missing person wanted to leave and where that person went.

Do children just wake up one day and decide to walk away from their parents? Rarely. It's sad, but most people I have talked to during my investigation stated that one or both of their parents—probably unknowingly—slowly drove them away. In many cases the parents had no idea how their daily behavior, attitudes, and choices were affecting their children.

You're probably asking yourself, how do I know if I'm driving my child away? From my experience we find the answers by searching for truth, by searching for honest answers.

Read through the following occupations and see if you can detect what they have in common:

- Detective: One employed or engaged in getting information that is not readily available or accessible.

- Private Detective: One employed by a private party to uncover truth in a specific situation.

- CIA: Central Intelligence Agency, uncovers data and possible threats. Agents collect intelligence by analyzing a steady flow of information.

- FBI: Federal Bureau of Investigation, FBI agents solve crimes on a national level.

- Information analyst: A retired FBI agent who legitimately sells information taken from all kinds of databases.

- Forensic scientist: A person who analyzes scientific data, such as DNA, with respect to legal matters.

- US marshal: A federal law enforcement agent charged with capturing fugitives.

- Bounty hunter: A private agent who gets paid for bringing in a fugitive.

- Toxicologist: A scientist who deals with the effects of poisons on living organisms.

If you figured it out, you just cracked your first case. They are all in search of answers; they are all in search of truth! They know that to be successful in their jobs they need to search every nook and cranny for truth. They don't have the luxury of denial. They have to push through the fear, do the painstaking work, and not worry about what others think about how they are doing their job. They know that if they don't find the bottom line—the truth—they won't find the answers they need. If people in these occupations know the importance of searching for truth, shouldn't we as parents be searching for truth in our relationships with our children?

Ancient Search
Investigators, or spies as they are sometimes called, have been around for several thousand years searching for truth.

> And the LORD spoke to Moses, saying: "Send men to spy out the land of Canaan, which I am giving to the children of Israel; from each tribe of their fathers you shall send a man, every one a leader among them."
> —Numbers 13:1–2

God knew it was important for Moses to see and understand what was happening around him. He didn't want him to stay in one place and bury his head in the sand. God wanted Moses to be aware, alert, wise, discerning. I have discovered this similar trait in courageous, successful parents. The deeper they look or spy out the land around them, the clearer the picture becomes. The dull areas in their relationships with their children become clearer, and they are able to make the necessary changes they need to build better relationships.

Then there's David's example. When David wrote Psalm 139, it was obvious he was on a desperate quest for truth. Ask yourself these questions:

> *O Lord, You have searched me and known me (v. 1).*
> Have I searched myself? Do I know myself? Do I know my children?

> *You know my sitting down and my rising up; You understand my thought afar off (v. 2).*
> Do I understand my thoughts? Do I understand my child's thoughts, even though I don't agree?

> *You comprehend my path and my lying down, and are acquainted with all my ways (v. 3).*
> Do I understand my ways, the paths I walk? Do I understand my children's ways, the paths they walk?

> *For there is not a word on my tongue, but behold, O Lord, You know it altogether (v. 4).*
> Am I aware of how I sound, what's coming out of my mouth? Am I truly listening to what is coming out of my children's mouths?

> *You have hedged [protected] me behind and before, and laid Your hand upon me (v. 5).*
> Do I hedge and protect myself by living with clear boundaries? Do I hedge and protect my children with clear boundaries I set for them?

> *Such knowledge is too wonderful for me; it is high, I cannot attain it (v. 6).*
> Do I understand how much God loves me? Do I understand how much God loves my children?

Where can I go from Your Spirit? Or where can I flee from your presence? (v. 7).

Do I run from His presence? Do my children run from His presence?

Indeed, the darkness shall not hide from You, but the night shines as the day; the darkness and light are both alike to You (v. 12).

I know I can't hide darkness from God, but am I hiding darkness from myself? Am I hiding from my kids' darkness, because it's too painful or I just don't want to deal with it?

Search me, O God, and know my heart; try me, and know my anxieties (v. 23).

Do I search myself and know my anxieties, worries, and fears? Do I know my children's anxieties, worries, and fears?

And see if there is any wicked way in me, and lead me in the way everlasting (v. 24).

Do I know what the wicked areas are in my life? Do I know what the wicked areas are in my children's lives? Do I allow God to lead me? Do I allow God to lead them?

Let's Be Honest!

Was it difficult to answer these questions? No matter what you answered, you are not alone. Remember, these questions are designed to help you look at yourself and your children more carefully, not make you feel bad about your parent/child relationship. When I present these questions at my FBI Parent Workshops, the usually chatty rooms become incredibly solemn. These questions provoke people to look deeper, to see if there are insights—things hidden—that they hadn't been aware of before. If you bravely and courageously contemplate these questions, it's a wise first step to understanding the heart of your child, as well as your own.

When My Daughter Walked Away

"Mom, I don't want to see you for a while," my grown daughter said nervously as she gazed down at her steering wheel. She wouldn't look me in the eye. She had called minutes earlier and told me she was on her way over and asked if I could meet her outside. "Come alone. I don't want to see or talk to Dad."

I was stunned. Maybe I should have seen this coming but her comment blindsided me. *What was she saying? Was she really cutting me and her father out of her life?* The rest of the conversation was like a slow-motion movie scene. I could hear her voice in the background but couldn't comprehend the words coming out her mouth. My mind was frozen, stuck on those ten little words, "Mom, I don't want to see you for a while." Ten little words I couldn't comprehend, "Mom, I don't want to see you for a while." *What did she mean exactly?*

I shivered, pulling my sweater close.

"What did I do?" I pleaded.

"It's just a lot of things," she said rubbing her brow. "Lots of things, one of them being that jealous thing you have with Laura." Laura is her mother-in-law.

My face grew hot, yet I felt numb.

"Heidi, I don't really think that I am jealous." Turning my head I gazed out the window. "I really don't know what you're talking about. It's not jealousy. It's that I don't understand where I fit in your life anymore."

"Whatever, Mom," she said rolling her eyes.

I hate that word *whatever*.

"Don't contact me for a while," she paused. "Ryan and I are going through some stuff, and we need to be alone."

Her words stung. She was cutting me off, and that meant cutting me off from my five precious grandkids. I stared at her, shaking my head, my eyes searching her face.

"OK, if that's what you want." I frantically reached for the door handle. I had to get out of her car.

"Mom, I love you," she said softly. Tears dripped down her face.

Yeah right, I thought angrily gripping the door handle. *It really seems like you love me.*

Dazed, I scooted out of the car. Gripping my stomach, I tried desperately to hold it together.

What was happening? Was she really banishing me from her life? In slow motion I staggered toward the front door of my condo, seven little words chasing me, "Mom, I don't want to see you. Mom, I don't want to see you." Ten more steps. *Just get to the door.* "Mom, I don't want to see you." *Maybe if I get away from her I can get away from this burning pain.*

How had our relationship come to this? I thought she loved me. What had I done wrong? I quietly opened the door, slipped inside and solemnly walked to my bedroom. Throwing back my white comforter, I slipped under the warmth and safety of my silky white sheets. Cradling my pillow I gave in to the pain that minutes earlier I desperately tried to corral. Strangely, the tears didn't come. I was in shock.

My husband came to the bedroom door. "Honey, it's almost noon. Why are you in bed? What's going on?"

"Heidi doesn't want to see us," I said peeking out from behind the pillow. "She told me to tell you not to contact her."

"Are you joking?"

"Honey, I'm telling you the truth. She said there are many issues—she and Ryan are going through some difficult things—and she doesn't want us to contact her."

"Did she say for how long?"

"No." One lone tear slid down my face.

Scratching his head he walked over and sat on the bed. "Tell me exactly what she said." He thought I was exaggerating.

"She said she doesn't want us to contact her. She doesn't want to see us for a while."

"You're joking. You're totally joking," he said frowning.

"No, I promise." I gulped. "I wouldn't joke about this."

His mouth dropped open. "I don't understand." His eyes searched mine. We stared at each other in icy silence as the immensity of our daughter's words began to sink in. This was our little girl. She wouldn't do this to us. We had been good parents. We had loved her, nurtured her…laid down our lives for her. We had gone without so she could have. I loved my daughter. Randy loved his "little punkin'."

Questions spilled from my mouth, "Why was she doing this to us? Had we been such bad parents? What is she thinking? Did we spoil her too much? What did we do wrong?" I felt dizzy, hurt, and angry. Those ten little words sent my husband and me into a tailspin of uncertainty, disbelief, and deep heartache.

My husband tried to lighten the mood, "Maybe she'll change her mind in the morning." I pulled the covers over my head and sobbed myself to sleep.

I woke up to a heavy, sinister cloud hovering over my head. Negative thoughts raged, fogging my mind, pinning me to the bed. *You're a terrible mother.* I couldn't get up. *You are such a bad person your daughter doesn't want to spend time with you.* I couldn't quiet my mind. *You're a terrible grandmother. You're a failure. Your own child hates you.* I gave myself a brutal mental beating. I was too weak to fight back.

Heidi ended up contacting us a couple of weeks later, and over a period of 18 months we began to restore our relationship. I didn't realize it at the time, but my daughter and her husband were going through a very difficult period. The choice for them not to see us was not so much about us, but about them. Her intentions weren't ever to hurt me.

Nevertheless, the process of reconciliation was slow and painful for me. It was a winding, blinding, exhausting journey of self-examination, as I struggled with rejection, denial, blame, forgiveness, and acceptance. I found it ironic that as I was working on this book about children walking away from their parents my own grown daughter walked out of my life. But through this experience I gained a deeper understanding of the tragedy and pain of losing a child, even if my loss was only temporary.

The Five Obstacles

As a result of my three years of investigative research and because of my own experience with my daughter, I discovered five reasons we as parents miss what is going on in the hearts of our children, our families, and ourselves:

1. Fear. I'm afraid to look at myself and my children. What happens if I discover things I don't know how to deal with? What if I'm to blame?

2. Pain. The truth is painful. Do I have the strength and wisdom to deal with it?

3. Image. The truth of how my children are behaving and the state of our family is embarrassing and shameful. What will others think?

4. Effort. I don't want to do the work; it's too hard; it requires too much from me. I don't want to change.

5. Denial. It's easier to live in a make-believe world than to face the truth.

Now let's use our investigative skills and bravely and courageously face these five obstacles head-on!

Obstacle #1:
Fear—God didn't give it to us.

Fear is deceptive. It can paralyze us; it can also cause us to panic and act unreasonably. Fear is an emotional obstacle that can, if we let it, keep us from the freedom God wants us to live in. *Merriam-Webster's 11th Collegiate Dictionary* gives a powerful definition of fear: "an unpleasant often strong emotion caused by anticipation or awareness of danger." Synonyms include: *dread, fright, alarm, panic, terror, trepidation.* Fear is an emotion that can rule our behavior. It can keep us from pursuing the hard answers we need to flourish in our relationships with our children. It's scary to look at ourselves, to truly admit how our behavior and attitudes affect those around us.

Most parents—myself included—wrestle with fear. When Heidi walked out of my life, I was fearful she would never come back. I was afraid to look at myself: what if the way I had raised her all those years was wrong? What if I had permanently damaged our relationship and it was irreparable? Fear hammered my emotions and caused me to panic and act unreasonably. I knew 2 Timothy 1:7 says, "*God has not given us a spirit of fear, but of power and of love and of a sound mind,*" but where could I find the power, the love, and the sound mind to deal with the fear? I felt powerless. When my daughter refused to see me, I didn't feel loving and my mind was anything but sound.

But then, as I went through this experience, I sought comfort in Psalm 91.

> *He who dwells in the secret place of the Most High shall abide [rest] under the shadow of the Almighty. I will say of the LORD, "He is my refuge and my fortress; my God, in Him I will trust."*
> —Psalm 91:1

The more I dwelt with God in the secret place, the less I feared. The more I abided (rested), the safer I felt. Through surrender and trust in God, I found power, love, and a sound mind. I knew He would sustain me. He became my sanctuary. He became my refuge. When fear snuck up on me and threatened to devour me, I imagined myself leaping into God's loving arms. And where did I find His loving arms? Friends, family, and most important, the Bible. I ran to His Word. I became empowered by the strength of Scripture. Proverbs 3:5–6 has become a favorite: "*Trust in the LORD with all your heart and lean not on your own understanding; in all your ways acknowledge Him, and He shall direct your paths.*"

Do you have faith that God is trustworthy and will sustain you? That He has you in the palm of His hand? Do you have faith that He won't give you more than you can handle?

Obstacle #2:
Pain—If it doesn't kill us, does it really make us stronger?

Sometimes, the truth is painful. It can be a pesky sting, like your friend telling you your child is disrespectful. Or a vicious bite, like a pastor encouraging you to take anger management classes. Sometimes it's absolute misery: your adult child telling you she wants nothing to do with you.

Pain is a part of life; it is unavoidable.

Beloved, do not think it strange concerning the fiery trial which is to try you, as though some strange thing happened to you; but rejoice to the extent that you partake of Christ's sufferings, that when His glory is revealed, you may also be glad with exceeding joy.
—1 Peter 4:12–13

I don't know about you, but I admit thinking that my pain often seems strange and unfair, and I am typically surprised when I am undergoing a fiery trial. I am more likely to have a shameless pity party for myself than graciously partake in Christ's sufferings. Like most people, I would rather avoid pain than endure it. But when it comes to my children, I am willing to deal with pain for the sake of the relationship. I would go through anything for them.

When Heidi walked away I was shocked and wounded. The intense pain provoked me to deep soul searching and prayer. I asked God to show me my faults. It was an excruciating process, but soon I understood that I did have some fault in her decision to walk away. I had to admit that my daughter pulled away because of how my behavior and attitudes affected her. An amazing thing happened: acknowledging and admitting what I had done wrong didn't kill me, it actually made me stronger.

During my initial research and now as I teach workshops, I have witnessed parents experience their deepest sorrows as they face the grief they had caused their children. It was painful for them to admit how their behaviors, attitudes, and choices had harmed their children. Inevitably, the courageous parents who endured the pain and answered the hard questions, were the ones who found the answers they desperately needed to connect or reconnect with the hearts of their children.

If there is any good news about pain, it is that pain almost always motivates us to change—if we let it. Are you ready to humble yourself and go through anything if it means building a stronger relationship with your child?

Obstacle #3:
Image—Do you see what I see?

I was scheduled to speak at a women's meeting one week after the fiasco with my daughter began. I was broken, beat up, and didn't think I'd have the strength to face anyone, let alone put on a happy face for women who needed encouragement. Even though I was writing a book and teaching workshops to help parents prevent their children from walking away, it happened to me. *God's little joke,* I thought.

So I considered quitting—afraid people would discover I didn't have it all together. My image as the perfect parent was shot! (I was only fooling myself anyway. My kids, friends, and husband already knew better.)

But now I see the experience with my daughter was probably the best thing that ever happened to me. I have deeper compassion and understanding for others, especially hurting parents.

Many families try to convey an ideal image—the perfect brownstone home, the latest fancy SUV, the most popular designer clothes. However, if these families were investigated, it wouldn't take a highly trained special agent to see that the perfect exterior doesn't match the condition of the families living inside. Steve and Jill lived in a prestigious neighborhood. Their children attended prominent schools. Steve held a high-status job and the family was held in high esteem in the community. When their children began getting into trouble, Steve and Jill made every effort to hide their children's behavior: after all, if they ignored the problems, perhaps they'd go away. This doesn't happen to the all-American Smiths, they reasoned.

We can't share honestly with others about what is happening in our family, they thought. *What will they think? It's easier living in our own little ideal world.*

Unfortunately they ignored the rumblings in the foundation of their home, until the entire facade collapsed. Steve and Jill divorced, and the children continued to ramble aimlessly down a dark road of destruction.

Do you sometimes try to portray a misleading image of your family? If we're honest, I think to some extent, we all do. I know I did, until the pain got so great, and it took too much work to hide. God is a gracious God; I discovered freedom by realizing that the only authentic image I truly wanted to portray was His! *"So God created man in His own image; in the image of God He created him; male and female He created them"* (Genesis 1:27).

Obstacle #4:
Effort—Are they worth it?

It's hard work to change. Most of us want our children to do the changing. After my daughter walked away, I knew that if I wanted to reconnect with her I was going to have to do the work, roll up my emotional sleeves, ease some of my expectations of her, and modify some of my behaviors.

Unfortunately, not all parents are up for doing the work. I see it over and over in my FBI Parent Workshops. Some parents figure it's easier to leave things the way they are—don't upset the applecart. These parents blame others, especially their children, for making bad choices, and they totally disengage from parenting. They rationalize it's easier to let their children figure out life for themselves. And often they just plain don't have the emotional or physical energy.

Kim and her brother were raised by a single mom. While answering questions in the FBI Parent Workshop, she discovered something disturbing.

"I was in junior high, and I didn't want to get outta bed," Kim shared as she brushed her dark hair from her eyes. "My mama walked in the room and told me, 'Get up!' I grunted and rolled over. She flashed me a disapproving glare and said, 'OK, if you don't wanna get outta bed to go to school, that's your problem.' She turned around, stomped through the door, and slammed it behind her. From that day on she never made me get up."

Kim and her younger brother both dropped out of school; she got into drugs and partying and eventually landed in a court-ordered drug rehabilitation center. Wiping tears from her cheeks she sobbed, "I wanted mama to care. I wanted her to make me get up. She just stopped parenting my brother and me. She was burnt out; she didn't want to do the work."

I know parenting can be tiresome and tedious, but have you ever thought of what it will cost you if you don't do the work? Can you trust God to give you the strength and courage to do the hard work it takes to find ways to connect to the heart of your child?

Obstacle #5:
Denial—Am I in denial? Not!

Initially, I thought my daughter was all wrong in her decision to cut her father and me out of her life. I was in denial that I had done anything wrong. Denial is a peculiar behavior. When you're in denial about something, you usually don't know it. Things may be completely obvious to people around you, but you are blind to them.

I was truly blind to the jealousy I felt toward Heidi's mother-in-law, Laura. But when I heeded Heidi's words, I really started looking at my heart and what I saw wasn't pretty. I had to begin looking at Laura with loving rather than condemning eyes. I then saw an entirely different person than the woman I wrongly perceived had stolen my daughter. Looking back I see clearly how for more than ten years I was jealous and acted rudely. Today, I consider Laura a friend.

In my research, I have interviewed many prisoners and parents of prisoners. Nearly every parent interviewed stated that they had been in denial of their child's destructive behavior for one or more of three reasons: they were too busy to deal with it, they didn't know what to do or they thought it was a phase and ignored the warnings.

Scott went from being a seemingly perfect son to being a prisoner. As the judge read the verdict, there were gasps in the courtroom. His dad began moaning; his mother burst into tears. Scott was sentenced to three years in the penitentiary for aggravated assault and battery. He was from an outstanding, prominent Christian family.

How could this happen? The answer lies in denial. For several years Scott's grandparents, other parents, close friends, and even the housekeeper, had tried to warn his parents of his deceptive behavior. But Scott's parents refused to see it, and the warnings fell on deaf ears. Unfortunately, their denial cost them dearly.

The problem with being in denial is you don't know it. You are blinded. You can't see reality, even if it lives under your roof.

In 2 Samuel 11:1–27, David set out on a downward spiral of deception when he looked down from his palace roof and saw Bathsheba bathing. He sent for her, lay with her, and she became pregnant. He then had her husband killed and took her as his wife. Then 2 Samuel 12:1–7 says the Lord sent Nathan to tell David a parable about a poor man who had nothing, except one little lamb, and a rich man who took the lamb to feed his hungry guest. David's anger was aroused and he said to Nathan, *"As the LORD lives, the man who has done this shall surely die! And he shall restore fourfold for the lamb, because he did this thing and because he had no pity."* Then Nathan said to David, *"You are the man!"*

How could David, who loved God so dearly—who was a man after God's own heart—do something so deceitful? Denial. Why didn't he see the error of his ways when it was so blatantly obvious to those around him? Denial. He had asked God to search him and know his heart, try him and know his anxieties, yet he hadn't searched his own heart and had obviously missed a blind spot.

If David could make such a huge mistake, is it possible that we as parents—who love our children so deeply—miss obvious keys in our relationships with our children? Are we open to exposing areas in which we are experiencing denial?

Since We're Digging, Let's Dig a Little Deeper!

We just learned how fear, pain, image, effort, and denial are all obstacles that keep us from discovering truth in our lives and in the lives of our children. But we're not finished yet: we need to dig a little deeper and understand why sometimes we need to search for truth in our pasts.

 Kid's Clue

"The art of communication is not what you can hear being said from the other person's mouth, but what you can feel from his heart and see in his eyes."
—Leah, 15
from *Wit and Wisdom from the Peanut Butter Gang* compiled by H. Jackson Brown, Jr.

CHAPTER 3

Beneath the Surface:

Digging into the Past Reveals Keys for the Future

Search me, O God, and know my heart; try me and know my anxieties.
—Psalm 139:23

How you make sense of your childhood experiences has a profound effect on how you parent your own children.
—Daniel J. Siegel and Mary Hartzell, *Parenting from the Inside Out*

Sometimes the keys to figuring out our children's needs lie in our own childhoods. You're probably wondering, *What does my childhood have to do with connecting with my children?* If we never make sense of our childhood experiences, the consequences are likely to affect our own children, whether we realize it or not. Daniel J. Siegel and Mary Hartzell explain it like this:

If you had a difficult childhood but have come to make sense of those experiences, you are not bound to re-create the same negative interactions with your own children. Without such self-understanding, however, science has shown that history will likely repeat itself, as negative patterns of family interactions are passed down through the generations.

—*Parenting from the Inside Out*

Having coached many parents, I have seen this to be true. People come into the workshop with either a chip on their shoulder toward their parents, or as soon as they left childhood they never looked back. Many who have had difficult childhoods don't even realize that they are carrying around baggage.

Siegel and Hartzell elaborate:

> When we become parents we are given an incredible opportunity to grow as individuals because we ourselves are put back into an intimate parent-child relationship, this time in a different role. So many times parents have said, "I never thought I'd do or say the very things to my children that felt hurtful to me when I was a child. And yet I find myself doing exactly that." Parents can feel stuck in repetitive, unproductive patterns that don't support the loving, nurturing relationship they envisioned when they began their roles as parents. Making sense of life can free parents from patterns of the past that have imprisoned them in the present.
>
> —*Parenting from the Inside Out*

Through observing and making sense of our past we can improve the present and our children's future. I wish I'd learned this truth when my children were little; however, I discovered it's never too late. I also discovered that making sense of my seemingly senseless past held some very important clues to restoration and healing.

Facing My Difficult Past

I was raised in a poor family with an alcoholic father. I grew up with an impending sense of doom. From as young as I can remember, I knew something was wrong. My father would come home drunk from work. My father wouldn't come home at all. My father would come home and be mad. My father would be brought home by the police. I would wake up in the middle of the night and look out my bedroom window to see the rain pounding and dad passed out in the driver's seat of the car. I was trained at a young age to expect dreadful things to happen daily, all the while never understanding it.

Most of my childhood insecurities revolved around our family car. We had an old, beat-up, forest green Chevy Biscayne station wagon with over 200,000 miles on it. It broke down weekly. When he wasn't at the bar, my dad would pound and scream at the car, dead in the driveway. He'd throw hammers and wrenches, yell at us kids to get out of the way, and cuss as though his tantrums would magically make the car start. On a good day, when it started, he would pack the family up in the station wagon—without mom who worked as a waitress at night—and head for the Clackamas River where he liked to fish and hunt. And then, you guessed it, the car would break down. Several times it ran out of gas, sputtering to a halt on the steep, winding curves to Estacada (fueling my fear of heights). Other times we'd have a flat tire on top of Goat Mountain where he took us to shoot guns (fueling my fear of guns). More than once I was stranded in our conked-out, 12-foot aluminum boat, the *Tagalong*, with night fast approaching and the company of one paddle, three siblings, our 80-pound black Lab, Satchmo, and a drunken dad. I've been lost and stranded on a desolate gravel road in the scalding heat of Eastern Oregon with not one but two flat tires and nothing to drink—but Dad had beer.

These unpredictable excursions fueled my insecurities. I have struggled daily throughout my life with an impending sense of doom. I describe "impending sense of doom" as waiting for the other shoe to drop, expecting something traumatic to happen on a daily basis. As a child, I lived holding my breath and shutting one eye, dreading what would happen next. Little did I know when I had children, I was carrying this impending-sense-of-doom behavior into my children's lives.

A few years ago I made this entry in my journal:

> Lord, You're showing me how fear of impending doom affected my parenting and many aspects of my life. I've been hyper-vigilant, making sure nothing uncomfortable ever happens to Heidi and Nicholas. I persistently harped on them in hopes of keeping them out of harm's way. I was a relentless nag. I did almost everything for them, because I didn't want them to experience pain. I figured the more I harped, the more control I had and the better they heard. Now, I see the more I harped the more they turned me off. I desired excessive control of their every move, so they wouldn't make mistakes. I didn't know how to let up. They're grown now Lord, and I see how this impending-doom thinking has affected the way I parented.

This fear not only affected my parenting but every area of my life. I struggled with a fear of becoming stranded, my car breaking down. I became panicky and unreasonable if I thought my gas gauge was getting low. When I walked out to my car, I checked to see if the tires were low. If I discovered they needed air, thoughts of impending doom sent me into a tailspin. If the car check-engine light came on or the car backfired I got angry, usually at my husband. But while journaling I had an incredible epiphany: Not one time in 27 years had my car ever broken down while I was by myself. No flat tire, no running out of gas; I had never been stranded.

I had a blind spot in my life, and I never saw it the entire time I was raising kids. I had parented my children with dark-colored, impending-doom glasses, and my irrational behavior drove them away from me. The sad thing is I knew my behavior was irrational, but I just didn't know why.

A New Take on My Childhood

For years—especially after I had children—I had a chip on my shoulder, *How could Dad have done this to me, to all of us kids?* For several years, every time I thought of my father my stomach would begin to churn. I felt like a helpless, shivering child alone and abandoned on a drifting boat. Depressive thoughts continually rolled over me like an early morning ocean fog: *He was a drunk who didn't care. He was selfish and did whatever he wanted. I'm never going to be like him. He didn't care about Mom or he would have spent time with her.* As the years went by the bad memories overshadowed any good, they colored the way I looked at life. I began to question, *Were there any good memories?*

A few years ago my husband and I went on a cruise to Alaska. *Wow, this is breathtaking,* I thought as I wrapped my arms around my knees and pulled the thick blue blanket tighter. *I had heard of the beauty of Alaska, but this goes way beyond what I imagined.* While the massive ship sliced through the still water in the majestic fjord, I was struck by the contrast of the towering white-capped mountains against the royal blue sky—it was simply breathtaking.

My eyes drank in the overwhelming beauty. I thought about how my dad loved nature. I was surprised as pleasant thoughts of my father began to surface: His arms around me as he showed me how to cast using a fly-fishing rod at Small Fry Lake. His pride in teaching me, his youngest daughter, to shoot a gun when I was six. The funny quacking sounds he made when ducks flew overhead. Making s'mores at Pelton Dam. Playing "I spy" while traveling to Montana. Tears began to trickle down my face as I remembered how his blue eyes danced when he saw a beautiful buck leap across the road during our car travels; the goofy grin that spread across his face as he clumsily danced with me standing on his feet; his infectious laugh at his own silly jokes. I remembered how I learned to sing four-part harmony with my brother and sisters in the back of the 1967 Chevy Biscayne station wagon while it weaved its way through the winding hills toward home from fishing expeditions. *My Dad would have loved this*, I thought to myself as I looked up and saw a bald eagle flying in the distance. As happy memories consumed my thoughts, my heart was flooded with love for my father, a love that I had long forgotten, suffocated by the painful memories of my childhood.

As the warm sun penetrated my chilled face, I whispered to God, "Why had I only remembered the bad memories of my father? Why had I allowed the good memories to be swallowed up by the bad?"

No answer. I knew this was a holy moment. I prayed.

> Heavenly Lord,
> Please forgive me for the embarrassment, shame, and anger I've harbored toward my dad. I release all of my hurt to You. I don't want to have negative thoughts toward him anymore. I let go of the pain he has caused me; I release him to You. I can see now how he was born with such a love of nature, animals, and people, but because of the choices he made and his alcohol use, he was robbed of reaching his God-given potential. I feel so sad for him and all that he lost. Thank You for letting me see Daddy through Your eyes, Lord. Thank You for reminding me of how much You loved him and grieved over him. Thank You for replacing the hatred I had for him with Your all-consuming love. Amen.

The day I stepped off the ship, I felt lighter, happier; life was simpler. My countenance changed. My thoughts shifted from what he had done to me and what I lost, to *"Poor Dad, look what he did to himself, and what he lost."* I had finally let Daddy off the hook. I forgave him. As I gained an adult perspective on my childhood I came to realize that he hadn't purposely set out to hurt his children. He loved us. He just lost himself and everyone else in his sickness. I had come to terms with my past, and I began to see things differently.

Can I Pass the Test?

When I arrived home from Alaska, I had to drive my car from Lake Havasu City, Arizona, to Las Vegas to have it serviced. I was driving my little car down I-40, where the speed limit is 75 mph and the semitruck drivers travel 80, playing a game of "dodge car" that I didn't want to play. While trying to maneuver out of their game, my car started to sputter. As I glanced in the rearview mirror I saw black smoke bellowing from the tailpipe. I pulled over to the side of the freeway, and my car died gliding to the shoulder.

I began panicking, *Oh no, what if one of those truck drivers hits me or worse yet, pulls over and kidnaps me. What if I die out here in the desert from dehydration? What if my cell phone won't work?* A cloud of doom settled over me. I needed to calm down. I started praying, asking God to help me, and suddenly remembered what I had written in my journal and started laughing. This is the impending doom I had been trying to avoid all my life. I started laughing. *This is a test. I'm not going to react like a helpless little child, because I am not a child anymore. I am not powerless over this situation. I am an adult, this is not hopeless,* I told myself. I picked up my cell phone and amazingly I had service. I called my husband, "Hi, honey, my car broke down. What should I do?" He called AAA and the tow truck was there in a half hour.

I did not get hit by a truck. I wasn't kidnapped. I didn't die of dehydration. I was victorious. Instead of being a victim, I was a victor. I had overcome a huge obstacle in my life, one that I hadn't even known was there. Sitting alongside the freeway waiting for the tow truck my eyes were suddenly opened. When I was a child I was helpless to doing anything when the car broke down and became despondent. But now, when those feelings of helplessness and doom threaten to paralyze me, I can rest in the fact that I am an adult and God has empowered me. I am not stranded without means to my own rescue.

More important for our children than merely what happened to us in the past is the way we have come to process and understand it. The opportunity to change and

grow continues to be available throughout our lives.
—Daniel J. Siegel and Mary Hartzell, *Parenting from the Inside Out*

It took a while, but I have processed and made peace with my past. I have gained understanding about my childhood. And I can honestly say that I now see that my childhood has molded me into the person I am today, and I'm content with that! It requires some hard work but I am retraining myself to respond differently to my children, imparting to them as well as myself, an everything-is-going-to-be-OK attitude instead of a beware-of-impending-doom attitude.

The Choice Is Yours!

I was a person who wasted a lot of time and energy blaming my dad, letting his bad choices affect my life even years after I moved out. True freedom came to me when I realized his bad choices motivated me to make better choices with my life. Unfortunately, my father died several years before I had this life-changing revelation.

How about you? Have you come to terms with your past? Have you integrated your past as part of your life story? Through my workshops I have heard countless horrendous childhood stories. Maybe your childhood was even more traumatic than mine. I am in no way downplaying the effects of sexual, emotional, or physical abuse. For some, coming to terms with their childhoods will take a lot more work than it did in my experience. I want to encourage you to seek out whatever or whomever it takes to make peace with your past: perhaps a great counselor, a pastor or wise friend. I've also provided many resources at the end of this book. What are you waiting for? Freedom is waiting!

Ready for More!

OK, now that you've used your God-given investigative courage and integrity to search for truth, the whole truth, and nothing but the truth, you are getting closer to uncovering what your child needs. You've searched your heart, overcome the five obstacles—fear, pain, image, effort, and denial—and you're still reading. You've bravely discovered the importance of searching for clues in your childhood and making peace with the past, with God's help. So, pat yourself on the back...you're now ready to follow the leads, find the missing links, and connect with your child!

Kid's Clue

"It's okay to have mean feelings, but don't be mean to others."
—Taylor Beyrent, 9
from *Never Eat Anything that Moves,* compiled and illustrated by Robert Bender

CHAPTER 4

Mission Possible:

How to Follow the Leads, Find the Missing Links, and Connect with Our Children

---

And my God shall supply all your need according to His riches in glory by Christ Jesus.
—Philippians 4:19

"Mommy," I bellowed from the rickety bottom bunk in my bedroom, "Come scratch my back!" No answer. "Mommm," I yelled growing agitated. Again, no answer. *OK, third time's the charm.* I let out a bloodcurdling scream, "Mommmy, come scraaatch my baaack!"

"Shhh," my sister said as she threw her head over the side of the top bunk, dangling her brown straggly hair in my face. "Don't be so loud. She'll come when she's ready."

I ignored her.

"Mom—Mom—Mom—Mom—Mom," I sounded like a chugging locomotive. "Mom—mom-mom-mom-mom-mom-mom..." I said gaining speed.

The sewing machine in the other room stopped. My chugging train came to an abrupt halt. I heard footsteps and soon Mom appeared in the doorway, her body silhouetted against the kitchen light.

"What are you screaming about?" she frowned, exasperated.

"Scratch my back; scratch my back!" I pleaded. I quickly scooted over. "Sit down, pleeease, Mommy, sit down," I begged. She wouldn't sit down. "Please, Mommy, sit next to me." I patted the sheet.

"No, honey. Go to sleep, you have to get up early. Besides I have sewing left to do." She said a quick prayer, stroked my back a few times, did the same to my sister and was gone.

As she walked out the bedroom door I imagined my words chasing her, stopping her flat in her tracks, grabbing her shoulders, making her do an about-face... hut one, hut two, hut three... and marching her back to my room: "Mommy, when I have kids I'm going to scratch their backs as long as they want." Soon I heard the buzz of the sewing machine; my words went unheeded.

Day after day, as I lay alone in my bed, I lulled myself to sleep by rehearsing that line over and over: "When I have kids I'm going to scratch their backs as long as they want."

My mother was a wonderful mother, and she met many of my needs; she just missed making an emotional connection with me at night. She worked as a waitress, had three other small children, an alcoholic husband, and survived in a state of exhaustion.

Discovering Each Child's Needs

Our children connect with people who meet their needs. If we as parents don't meet their needs, they will bond with someone who does. Our job is to find and meet our children's needs!

In my case, it wouldn't have been hard for my mother to discover what I needed, because I shouted it from my bunk bed. However, because of different temperaments, many children are more difficult to read. My sister had a quiet temperament and internalized her needs—she was considered the good child. Unfortunately, many of her needs as a child went unmet and undiscovered, because everyone assumed she was fine. She never told them otherwise.

While I've encouraged you to search every nook and cranny for truth, there's one area not to search in—formulas! If you're looking for the perfect formula to raise or reconnect with your child, you're not going to find it. There is no perfect method for raising your child. As great detectives know, just when you think you have the perfect formula figured out, something happens to blow that formula to smithereens. As each child's temperament is different, the method in which you reach your child's heart will be different as well.

In their book *The Power of Teachable Moments,* Jim Weidmann and Marianne Hering stress the importance of understanding each of our children's personalities and being tuned in to their emotions.

To encourage, you need to understand where your kids are emotionally. Every child is different. You have to be sensitive to different personalities and make sure you know what's going on emotionally with a particular child. What energizes one will break the spirit of the other. To encourage them with empathy, you have to know how to read them, and sometimes you fail.

When you are able to offer empathy to your child, you are sensitized to his or her feelings, and you know when to be strong, when to share, when to speak those hard truths, and when to simply listen.

—Jim Weidmann and Marianne Hering, *The Power of Teachable Moments*

Your job as investigator isn't to discover some magic formula, but to make discoveries specific to your child's heart. Formulas don't work. Being sensitive to your child does.

Stop and ask yourself these questions: Is my child easy to read? Do I understand his or her individual needs? Is it possible he or she has hidden needs? If my child isn't so easy to read, how can I discover possible missing links and connect to his or her heart?

Special agents use many clever methods to find missing links. Parents can learn a lot from the agents' expertise. As I mentioned in chapter 2, they use extensive questioning; read body language; use their senses; make timelines; backtrack; dissect minute, seemingly insignificant details; and use many investigative resources. Now before you call in the bounty hunter because you think I've lost my investigative mind, stick with me. By using similar techniques—methods I call the "four FBI parenting tactics"—you will discover surprising and revealing things about yourself and your children. You will find your children's needs.

The Four FBI Parenting Tactics

The four FBI parenting tactics are: identifying the struggle; thoughtfully questioning and contemplatively listening; observing body language and countenance; and using your senses. Let's examine each one separately.

Parenting Tactic #1:
Identifying the Struggle

One of the first things a detective does when he's given an assignment is to identify the problem. We as parents need to identify the areas in which we struggle with our children. What are those areas of struggle in your relationship with your child? Maybe your child doesn't listen, is unresponsive, acts disrespectfully, or flat-out doesn't connect with you.

I was coaching a woman I'll call Carol. One day she shared how frustrated she was with her seven-year-old son, Cory. "He drives me crazy. Last night I was trying to help him study the spelling words, and he got mad and yelled at me." After a few seconds she went on, "He doesn't respect me."

I nodded, "Tell me where the frustration and struggle is in your relationship."

Tears began to well in her eyes. "Everything, just everything," she admitted ashamed. "We clash the minute he wakes up in the morning."

As I further investigated, Carol disclosed that she is a high achiever and perfectionist, and she is rarely satisfied with her young son's accomplishments. Unconsciously, she had conveyed to him: *Try harder. You have to keep up with the other kids. There is no room in our family for second best. You have to be the best.* Cory began to withdraw and disconnect from his mother—she was too intense. He had a need for acceptance and trust from his mother, but it went unmet.

However, Cory was deeply attached to his father. He respected him and worked hard to please him, because Dad made things fun and didn't nag. After all, his father accepted him just the way he was.

"When you pick up Cory from school, what do the tone of your voice and your eyes say?" I asked. She thought for a minute, "They convey desperation, panic, and probably anger, 'Did you pass that spelling test?'"

"So your first comment to Cory isn't, 'Hi, honey, how was your day?' but 'Did you pass the spelling test?'"

She was quiet, tears began to form again. "Wow, I never saw this before. I never looked at it that way."

"Do you think that when Cory is around you he feels like a failure?"

"Probably," she sniffled.

"Carol, your son needs to feel accepted by you. He has a need to trust you to support him, but all he is getting is 'You're a failure.' The best thing you can do for your child is focus on his heart, not on his performance. His heart is good. He feels pressure, because he's not measuring up. He may even feel panic, like everyone is getting it, and he isn't." In deep thought we both stared at each other.

"Imagine Cory in a boat by himself trying to paddle around a lake. He's never been in this boat. He doesn't know how it works, doesn't even know how to put the paddles in the oarlocks. In the back of his mind he's praying he won't tip over the boat, because he barely knows how to swim. He's a little scared but trying to be brave. He keeps looking to the shore for reassurance from you and your husband. You're standing on the shore screaming, 'Dip the paddle. Paddle more with your left arm. Paddle faster, now paddle slower. I told you to put the paddles in the water.'"

He becomes overwhelmed, throws down the paddles and starts screaming at you. Meanwhile, Bob, his dad, is standing calmly on the shore *observing* his son. He believes Cory has what it takes to figure it out. When Cory looks at his dad he doesn't see rage, disappointment, or frustration; he sees reassurance, delight, admiration, and confidence. He shuts you out but desperately looks to his father for guidance, 'Daddy, will you help me?'"

"I love my son; I want the best for him," Carol pleaded.

"I know that, but is that what your behavior is telling him? Do you think Cory knows? How do you think you can take the struggle out of your relationship?" I asked.

"By focusing on his heart and not so much on his accomplishments," Carol replied.

Because Carol identified the struggle and began to look at her son differently, she came to understand him better and he became more responsive and loving. Over time Carol learned to focus more on who Cory was and less on what he did.

Parenting Tactic #2:
Thoughtfully Questioning and Contemplatively Listening

Asking questions and listening to the responses are two of the most important investigative methods used by detectives. Similarly, parents can learn to use questioning and contemplative listening to identify struggles with their children and gain priceless wisdom and insight.

Remember Katie Harman, the young woman mentioned in chapter 1 who became Miss America 2002? Katie's parents, Glen and Darla, discovered an important secret that created a bond with their children. Fortunately for them, they discovered it at a pivotal time in their children's lives.

"When Katie and her sister, Stacey, were about 10 and 12 years old, we were extremely active working in the church. Busyness had taken over my life," Katie's mom, Darla, shared.

"One day Glen and I felt impressed by God to turn off the television and unplug the phone and get to know our children. It was a pivotal point in our parenting, because how can we raise them if we don't know them?"

She explained that at first she and her husband sat down with their children twice a week to have a Bible study at home.

"We had our first meeting, and both of the girls hated it; it was a flop. For two weeks we struggled through these meetings—much to the dismay of the girls." Darla went on, "I became increasingly frustrated, which brought me to pray: 'God the girls are miserable; Glen and I are miserable. It's obvious this isn't working.'"

After a few minutes of quiet she sensed, "I never told you to have church—I said get to know your children."

Aha, thought Darla, *that's what the problem is.* In the next few days Darla and Glen put together a three-page questionnaire that asked general questions about their faith. For example: What does going to church mean to you? What does this Bible verse mean to you? Who is God? Why do we get baptized? What are the four spiritual laws?

"There are no right or wrong answers," Darla explained. "We just want to know what you know, so be as honest as you can. You will never be in trouble for what your opinions and answers are."

It wasn't long before the Bible questions evolved into questions about all aspects of life. Three times a week the family would sit down together, usually after dinner and discuss a whole host of questions. No topic was ever off limits: What does it mean to be successful? If your friend stole some gum from the store what would you do? If you were at a party and you saw someone taking drugs what would you do?

• *The Art of Listening*
Through this process, Darla and Glen bonded deeply with their girls. They came to know their children—their deepest dreams and desires. They actively listened (nodded their head, gave direct eye contact) to their children's opinions and fears,

and they learned what they thought about many things. Because Darla and Glen didn't laugh, scoff, or put down their daughters' thoughts and opinions, their daughters' trust in them grew (see clue #1, chapter 5), a trust that bonded them even more deeply as the years went by. Because the girls felt heard (see clue #2, chapter 6), they felt valued (see clue #3, chapter 7) and respected. Through the hundreds of discussions they had together over the years the family defined what was truly valuable and found the importance of boundaries. Did you get that? They had discussions, not lectures. Together they dissected subjects. Because they knew their girls individually, Darla and Glen knew how to give them appropriate boundaries (see clue #4, chapter 8). Because these boundaries were fair and consistent, the girls gradually embraced similar boundaries for themselves.

Another clue Darla and Glen discovered was that by shutting their mouths and intentionally listening to their daughters they picked up on specific ways the girls needed to feel supported (see clue #5, chapter 9) and helped both of them discover choices they could make to give their lives purpose and meaning (see clue #6, chapter 10).

• *Let's Get Real*

Katie and Stacey got to know their parents more deeply as well during the conversations, because their parents answered the same questions they did. Darla and Glen shared openly with them about their successes as well as failures; thus they became more approachable to their girls.

"Glen and I became real people to them, not just someone they put on a pedestal," says Darla.

Because they bravely opened up to their children about their concerns, disappointments, and struggles in life, their daughters looked at them as genuine people, not "know-it-all, perfect parents." They could relate and talk more freely with them.

For some silly reason parents think they have to "have it all together." But that's simply not true. In *A Dad-Shaped Hole in My Heart*, H. Norman Wright writes, "A father who is honest with his daughter about his own flaws becomes her confidant." Had Katie's parents ignored that pivotal chance to get to know their children, their needs, and their search for truth, it's quite possible the outcome of their children's lives might have been very different.

• *Just Ask*
While attending a dance-team workshop, I noticed a large group of teenage students congregating around Mrs. Gray, a heavyset, graying, middle-aged schoolteacher. As I observed them giggling and laughing, I could tell they shared a special camaraderie. She was teaching a class later in the day, and I decided I wanted to hear what this teacher had to say.

During the question-and-answer period a parent asked Mrs. Gray why she had such a special relationship with her students. How could she possibly make them all feel so special? She lowered her head and sheepishly grinned, "Everyone thinks I'm so smart, but I'm not. I just simply ask really good questions." You could hear a pin drop.

Questions? You ask really good questions? I thought to myself. *Well why didn't I think of that... probably because I am usually too busy talking.*

Her voice interrupted my thoughts, "I rarely say anything. I just listen, and everyone thinks I'm so smart." She had learned the art of asking questions. "My students feel I care about them, because I ask them their opinions. I don't necessarily agree, I just listen!"

• *Motives?*
Before moving on to some FBI questions, I want to say it's important to examine our motives for asking questions. Is it to interrogate our children, to find something wrong in their thoughts or behavior? To see if they give us the right or wrong answers? Or is it to truly understand how they think and feel about things? Remember, before questioning it's important to examine your motives!

FBI Questions

1. Do you consider yourself a good listener? Do others consider you a good listener?

2. Do you find yourself lecturing more often than having family discussions?

3. When your child is talking, are you already formulating your response, or are you truly trying to grasp what he is saying?

4. Is it possible that you are missing important clues to reaching the heart of your child because you aren't listening?

5. Do you find it easy to talk to your child? Why or why not?

6. Do you think your child finds it easy to talk to you?

7. Are you open about your past failures? Why or why not?

8. Are you open about your past successes? Why or why not?

9. Are you open about present successes and failures? Why or why not?

10. Do you share openly about your childhood? Why or why not?

11. Do you share openly about your views on education?

12. Do you share openly your thoughts on God? What about other spiritual issues?

Parenting Tactic #3:
Observing Body Language and Countenance

Those who look to him are radiant; their faces are never covered with shame.
—Psalm 34:5 (NIV)

Detectives know that a person's countenance and their body language are often dead giveaways to many things that go unsaid. A suspect's words can say one thing, but his countenance and body language can tell a completely different story. We can make similar discoveries in our lives and the lives of our children.

• *Countin' on Our Countenance*
Perry and Margaret were desperate to find ways to connect with their child. As they walked into the church chapel, I noticed their stunning height contrast: Perry is a handsome, African American man who towers a full 14 inches over his 5-foot, 100-pound wife, Margaret. Her gorgeous black hair, highlighted with flecks of gold, was braided gloriously like a crown around her head. Her beautiful brown eyes danced as her infectious smile lit up the room.

She is from Zimbabwe; he is from the United States. When they married two years earlier, they gained custody of his son from a previous relationship. Margaret and Perry had recently had a baby girl of their own, and as the baby grew, Perry's son became increasingly out of control. The school was pressuring them to put him on medication. The church was exasperated with nine-year-old Michael and didn't want him attending Sunday school classes. When he was home he was somewhat compliant, but the minute he left home they were getting calls about his disruptive behavior.

They approached me for ideas after meeting me at a marriage workshop I was teaching. I explained to them that I wasn't a professional counselor, but I would be happy listen.

After talking with them for several minutes I discovered Margaret was clueless about how to balance this new life, with an out-of-control nine-year-old and her one-year-old baby. Perry was at wit's end, feeling hopeless and confused as to how to keep his new family in sync.

Finally I asked, "What does your countenance say to your son when you're around him?"

"What do you mean by *countenance*?"

"Does your face light up when you see him, or are you glaring at him?"

"Hmmm," I could see Perry's mind ticking away.

"What does Michael see in your eyes when he observes you watching his new baby sister?"

Both of their eyes instantly lit up. "Delight," they said without hesitating.

"Does he see that she brings you happiness and joy?"

"Yes, definitely."

"He sees your eyes light up when she is around. What does he see in your eyes when he walks into a room?"

They both got really quiet.

"Probably shame, grief, and disappointment," Perry said shyly.

As we talked further, they began to realize that their precious son not only feels like a disappointment to them, but to his teachers at school, to his mother who isn't raising him, to his friends' parents, and to the Sunday School leaders. He is carrying a huge burden of disappointment. He probably has a huge bubble over his head that says, "I'm a loser," and he sees it in everyone's eyes.

I spoke of the six clues and explained all six to them. They decided that he's having a difficult time trusting and doesn't feel understood or valued by them, or anyone else for that matter.

"Does he ever see the delightful, fun, childlike side of you?" I asked Perry.

"No, probably not," he paused. "He just sees the strict, serious side."

"He needs to see that he isn't a disappointment to you—that you love and delight in him as much as you do his little sister. He needs to be valued by being unconditionally loved by you," I said. "He has a need to feel special to someone in his life. He needs to feel as special as his little sister."

After several minutes of brainstorming, Perry and Margaret decided that they were going to begin "dating" their son. They would set apart special times when they would make it "his day," focus on him, and talk about and actively listen to his interests. He would have time alone with his new stepmom without the baby, and he would have time alone with his daddy. They both agreed that their job was to change the bubble over his head from "I'm a disappointment" to "I'm a delight."

As Margaret and Perry became aware of what their countenance was saying to their son, they made a conscious choice to change it. It took work, but as their son grew he began to see more approval and delight in his daddy's eyes, fewer glares of doom and disappointment. He felt valued, because he felt heard. Margaret's countenance changed from confusion to understanding. Because he felt accepted, Michael opened up about his doubt and insecurities and settled down in other areas of his life.

Margaret and Perry began building a new relationship with Michael by changing the way they related to him. By taking a hard look at what their countenance and body language were saying they found a key to his heart.

Just as the painful image of a parent standing hand on hip with a pointing finger and disapproving glare stays with a child long into adulthood, so does the loving embrace and approving smile of a proud parent. Clues to connecting with the hearts of our children are found in our glowing smiles not in harsh stances and glaring frowns. What does your face say to your children? What is your body language saying? Ask yourself these questions.

FBI Questions

1. When you think of your father, do you remember his eyes showing delight or disapproval when you walked into a room?

2. When you think of your mother, do you remember her eyes showing delight or disapproval when you walked into a room?

3. What does your countenance say to your children?
   - "I delight in being with you?" or "I am disappointed in you?"
   - "I'm too tired to deal with you?" or "I always have time for you?"
   - "I'm exasperated with you?" or "I'm exhilarated when I'm with you?"
   - "I'm disgusted with you?" or "I'm proud of you?"

Parenting Tactic #4:
Making Sense of the Senses

Investigators and spies have been using their five senses since the beginning of time. God gave our senses to us so we could fully experience life—its beauty as well as its hazards—by seeing, hearing, tasting, touching, and smelling. As detectives know, if they only engage one of their senses, they will miss other vitally important clues in their search for the truth. If on the other hand, they engage all five of their senses, they gain a better understanding of what is happening around them and have a better chance of discovering possible missing links.

• Experiencing Life to the Full
My friend Suzi Sanford's life was tragically cut short because of cancer. She was an incredible mother to two daughters and had a heightened awareness of her surroundings: the enticing smell

of milk chocolate rippling through the air; the high-pitched sound of wind breezing through her window at night; the soft, gentle touch of her ten-year-old daughter's hand clasped safely in hers; her dancing taste buds as she savored the taste of chocolate cheesecake. She lived in the moment, because, toward the end of her life, she didn't know how many more moments she would have.

She was also incredibly aware of the negative side to heightened senses. The putrid hospital smell where she got her chemotherapy; the taste of bile that accompanied her treatments; the pain she endured as she was pricked with needles; and the agony she saw in her husband Tim's eyes as he sat helplessly watching her life slip away.

God gave us the gift of our senses to experience life and death. He wants us to be aware of how fleeting our life is and how fleeting these years of parenting are, so that we can live richer lives and have deeper relationships. He wants us to live in the moment.

Therefore I tell you, do not worry about your life, what you will eat or drink; or about your body, what you will wear. Is not life more important than food, and the body more important than clothes?
—Matthew 6:25 (NIV)

Have you ever considered how God gave us our senses to give us insight into the hearts of our children and loved ones? God gave us touch, sight, smell, taste, and hearing to experience and enjoy the delightful things our children are doing and to warn us when something just isn't quite right. When we use our senses we see things we've never seen before, the good and the bad.

When my children were small I was sensitive to their baby powder smells, their precious little gurgles, the times they rolled over, but as time went on it wasn't so precious. It became hard work. Busyness in life has a way of trying to take over: making lunches; putting dinner on the table; not to mention doing the laundry, keeping clean sheets on the beds, and getting the kids to school or home schooled.

I have to admit, when my children were little, I thought it was going to last forever. I reasoned: time is on my side. I truly didn't realize how fleeting it was! I missed incredible moments, because I was tired and my senses had dulled. I cringe at the times I missed, because I didn't see the delight in my daughter's eyes as she was trying to show me a potato bug or the moments I missed because I didn't hear the beautiful giggles streaming from the backyard as Heidi and Nicholas splashed in the pool. It grieves me to think of how I'd try to shake my daughter from my leg as her tiny little hands would gently tap me on the bottom trying to get my attention. She had something important to tell me, but because I was on the phone with a friend I missed her precious discovery.

Be sensitive to your children by using your senses: smell the fragrance of your child's hair when you lift her out of the tub; touch your teen's shoulder as he passes you to get a soda; gaze at your toothless child as he belly-laughs while watching you be goofy; try to appreciate the taste of bubble gum ice cream if your toddler wants to share; and above all, listen with both your ears and your heart.

Time is fleeting. Tune into your children before they tune you out!

You're Almost There!

You've just learned how to connect to the heart of your child by using the four FBI parenting tactics: identifying the struggle; asking questions and contemplatively listening; paying attention to body language and countenance; and using your God-given senses! By using these four tactics you are well on your way to discovering how to be emotionally, spiritually, and physically connected to your children, building strong bridges to their hearts.

From the Heart of an Investigator

I have to admit that my inconsistencies and inadequacies while raising my kids felt like neon signs flashing my failures: "Didn't ask enough questions!" "Didn't give them my undivided attention!" "Impatient!" "Intense!" "Talked too much!" "Listened too little!" "Yelled when I should have laughed!" "Glared disapprovingly when they needed me to teach them lovingly!" "Embarrassed them when I should have embraced them!"

I was—and still am—anything but perfect. However, if my heart instead of my actions were a billboard, it would read: "She loves her children and would never intentionally set out to hurt or harm them in any way!"

I thank God for His grace. I don't deserve it, but He gives it to me anyway. Without His help and grace I am hopeless. I am so grateful that early on in my parenting years, when I felt so incredibly inadequate, I learned to run to Him. As Job 10:12 states, *"Thou hast granted me life and favor, and thy visitation hath preserved my spirit"* (KJV). He has visited me when I was so utterly exhausted I couldn't lift my head off the pillow, and when I was so exasperated with myself and my children that I could barely stagger to Him. He visited me when I got on my knees and cried out to Him.

"I am so incapable of raising these kids."

"I know," He'd whisper. "I *am* capable; look to Me and I will make you capable."

The flashing lights of my failures did illuminate my weaknesses, however, after my children were raised I came to realize that my failures as a parent weren't as bright and as obvious as I had imagined. The realization came through an unexpected gift I received a few years ago from my grown daughter. Here's the note she gave me:

Mom,

I was tucking Joshua [four] in tonight and Rachel [two]. First, I was lying with Rachel and worshipping, and she was worshipping too. She was repeating whatever I sang, and I was playing with her hair. Afterward, I went to tuck Joshua in. I asked him, "Joshua, do you want to worship with me?" And he did. We started singing, "Jesus, Jesus, Jesus, there's just something about that name…"

I kept trying to remember what you did that made that so special when I was little and growing up. I remember you always worshipping and rubbing the back of my head. It was one of the most secure and happiest feelings I ever had. You gave that to me and in a way, gave that to my kids, because I would probably not do it had you not done that with us. I don't think I do it as well as you did, but I hope my kids will be as impacted by it as I was.

It's not just that you would sing with me, but you taught me to worship, and you set aside your night to worship with me. I am so thankful for the mother you were while I was growing up, now that I have my own kids. I can look back and remember the things you did with us and the way you were with us and be that to my own kids. I am so thankful for you and your influence in my life. I love you so, so, so much and pray continually for God's blessing and perfection on your life. I could not ever give you back what you have given me in my life. Thank you, Mom.

I love you, more than you could know,
Heidi Lee

Because my need to have my back scratched as a child went unmet, when I had children I purposed to give them what I had wanted as a child. So, from the time they were tiny infants, I spent at least 30 minutes talking with each of my children as I tucked them in. I would press my face against my daughter's tiny soft face and sing over and over, "Jesus Loves Me." As she grew, she began singing with me, "Jesus, Jesus, Jesus, there's just something about that name…" (We joke that when she was an infant she had perfect pitch.) She sang melody, and I sang harmony. By the time she was four she was singing harmony. I would do the same with my son.

Our worship times evolved into sweet godly encounters as my children grew. No matter how crazy things were during the day, I think they both knew that when night came Mom would calm down, they would have my undivided attention, and together we would experience the presence and peace of God.

Regardless of my perceived failures as a parent, my children turned out to be loving individuals. They are both grown now and work in ministry and music. My son has a small recording studio and is also a worship leader at church. My daughter has written hundreds of worship songs, plays piano, and is also a worship and youth leader.

Now that is the grace of God!

Kids' Clues

"When someone loves you, the way they say your name is different. You just know that your name is safe in their mouth."
—Billy, 4

"I know my mommy loves me, because she scratches my back at night."
—Trinity Heinsohn, 6, my granddaughter

PART TWO:

SOLVING THE MYSTERY—THE SIX CLEVER CLUES

The true mystery of the world is the visible, not the invisible.

—Oscar Wilde

CHAPTER 5

Get a Clue #1
To Trust or Not to Trust,
That Is the Question

Uncovering your child's
need to trust and
to feel safe and secure

It is impossible for God to lie,...this hope we have as an anchor of the soul, both sure and steadfast.
—Hebrews 6:18–19

More than what the parents say, the child stores how the parents *are* in the world.
—Harville Hendrix and Helen LaKelly Hunt, *Giving the Love that Heals*

As any good detective will tell you, assuming something is true when it's not is the worst mistake to make on any case. When I began this investigation, I assumed I knew the primary reason children disconnected and walked out of their parents' lives. However, after a poolside conversation during a vacation in Mexico, my seemingly concrete assumptions cracked and crumbled into a million little pieces.

Mindful in Mexico

"Are you raising your children the same way you were raised?" I asked a husband and wife sitting in the lounge chairs next to me.

"Why?" the wife asked cautiously.

"I'm doing research for a book I'm writing about why children walk away from their parents' values and convictions," I said, chewing on my lip.

She pointed at her husband, "I wasn't raised in a religious home, but he was; talk to him." And she left.

Obviously, she wasn't going to answer me, but he stayed put.

"I was raised strict Baptist. My parents had us five kids in church every time the doors were open." He paused, "Almost every day of the week. To answer your question, my boys, ages 18 and 13, have never been to church in their lives."

He seemed angry.

Whoa, I thought to myself, *he's eager to tell his story.* I pulled my lounge chair closer. "Why?"

"I would never subject my boys to what I went through as a kid. My dad was so mean to my mother. He loathed her. They squabbled constantly. They were verbally abusive to each other," he scratched his head. "Dad wasn't a happy man."

"When he wasn't fighting with Mom, he had us out in the garage whoppin' us. 'Quit being babies. Wipe your tears. Get in the car. Church starts in ten minutes.'

"All the way to church he would belittle my mother. She'd glare at him. We'd show up at the church doorstep, five cowardly kids, my mother nervously rubbing her hands together, and my father's scowl would be replaced by a humongous comic smile like the Joker from the *Batman* movies. But it was no joke. I vowed to never live like them, and that included church. When I left home, it was a no-brainer, I left their beliefs."

Mark's wasn't an isolated case. You probably already know that; maybe you even grew up in a similar situation. Over the course of several weeks, I asked many more people the same question and began tallying data.

Interview after interview confirmed that how parents treat each other has a huge impact on the children. Are you following that? How we parents (married or divorced) relate to each other deeply affects our children.

As it turns out, based on my research, the number one reason children emotionally, physically, or spiritually walk away from their parents isn't because the parents were preoccupied with work, life, and church as I had assumed. Instead, children walk away because they grew up observing tension, hostility, or fighting between the parents on a daily basis and didn't develop a sense of trust toward them. Children also disconnected if they observed their parents being unkind or disrespectful to each other on a regular basis; if they saw their parents were inconsistent and unreliable; and if the parents weren't transparent and honest about their mistakes, struggles, failures, but rather projected a "perfect" persona when the kids knew otherwise.

What's Driving Our Kids Away? Us.

When children observe parents being dishonoring and disrespectful to one another, it causes serious damage. Here are a few comments made by adult children in my workshops:

> "Sure, my parents didn't lie openly to me, but how they acted and what they said were two different stories: 'You need to be loving to your sister,' and then they'd turn right around and be unloving to each other. It was very confusing."
> —Kevin

Kevin felt that his parents were always pitted against each other, which put him in the uncomfortable position of choosing sides. He felt like a Ping-Pong ball. If one parent would treat the other negatively, he felt as if he had to defend the other. He lived in constant turmoil as to which side to take. It was an awful lot of pressure for a little boy.

"My parents said they loved each other, but when my mom wasn't around, my dad would make negative comments about her: 'You know your mother; maybe if she quit spending money I wouldn't have to work so much and could spend more time with you kids.' On the other hand, my mother would say: 'You know your father; if he wasn't such a workaholic he'd spend time with us.'"
—Caroline

"As a child I felt like I was a little mouse hiding in a cage with two rats. My parents were so busy running around nipping at the other they didn't notice me cowering in the corner or notice how their behavior affected me. I wanted out of that cage. I thought when they got divorced it would get better, but nothing has changed. They never see or talk to each other, but they bad-mouth each other through me. I feel awful because I hate to be around them; for my sanity I avoid them at all costs."
—Susan

"My parents were like two ships passing in the night. They didn't fight, but it was obvious they didn't like each other because they never spent any time together. Looking back, it seemed they were avoiding each other."
—Kyle

Several adult children of divorced parents shared the same sentiment: "My parents were disrespectful to one another—who was I going to side with? My loyalties were with both parents. They are the two people I love most on this earth; it was very confusing."

Be Honoring and Respectful...No Matter What

The number one reason, in my investigation, that children walked away was because parents didn't honor and respect one another. When we honor and respect our child's other parent, we honor the child. When we dishonor and disrespect the other parent, we dishonor and disrespect the child.

Early in my marriage, I talked down to my husband, not just with harsh words but a nasty tone of voice, glaring eyes, and a ridiculous scowl on my face. Randy didn't appreciate it and lovingly set me straight, "Please don't talk to me like that; you sound like you hate me. Would you talk to your friends like that?"

He shocked me. "No, I guess not," I said.

"I used to have to listen to my mother talk to my father like that and I'm not going to listen to you." He remembers how his father's countenance would change at his mother's spiteful words. It hurt Randy deeper than it hurt his dad, because he esteems his father dearly.

I thank God that Randy taught me early in our marriage how to treat him, by not allowing me to talk down to him. When I honor my husband, I honor my children.

When we feel honored, we feel respected. When we honor others—our spouses, friends, family, co-workers, and children—with kind words, considerate actions, and helpful attitudes, they feel loved and respected, and if we do this consistently we develop a trusting relationship. However, if we dishonor and disrespect others we are actually breeding mistrust. If our children don't trust us, they will find someone to trust. Who will it be?

Dean Ornish, MD, in the book *Big Shoes: In Celebration of Dads and Fatherhood,* shares this insight about his family:

> My natural inclination is to trust people until proven otherwise, because I come from a loving, trusting family...Of course, you get hurt at times when you go around with an open heart, but if your heart is closed, it's much harder to connect with people. And trust, more than any other single place, comes from the kind of relationship that you have with your parents.
> —Al Roker and friends, *Big Shoes*

At the core of every child is a need to trust. Trust is either built or destroyed through what children observe in our behavior toward them and others. Why do children need a strong sense of trust? Because their entire emotional, physical, and spiritual foundation is built on it. If their foundation is built on honesty and integrity, our children will feel safe and secure, and they gain assurance that everything will be OK.

Cracks in their foundation are created when our children see us dishonoring or disrespecting their other parent, others, or themselves; when we lack humility and don't own up to our own failures and struggles; and when we are unreliable and inconsistent.

Our children don't miss a beat! They are like little video cameras, observing and recording our every move, action, and attitude, storing them on a daily basis. They are constantly downloading how you treat their daddy or mommy; how you act toward the guy who cut you off; the tone of your voice when you talk about their grandma; if you are reliable and hold to your word; and if you are honest. Those tapes are often indestructible and aren't easily erased.

Behold, how good and how pleasant it is for brethren to dwell together in unity!
—Psalm 133:1

FBI Questions:
Uncovering Clues in Your Childhood
Let's see what you remember from your life as a child.

1. Did your parents honor *each other* when you were a child?

2. Did their relationship positively or negatively effect you?

3. Did you trust your father? Your mother?

4. Did you grow up feeling safe and secure?

5. Do you have a hard time trusting men? Do you have a difficult time trusting women?

6. Were your parents reliable? Were they consistent? Did they do what they promised?

7. Did you run from your parents' lifestyle, values, and convictions?

8. What kind of relationship do you have with your parents now?

9. Are you naturally trusting or distrusting?

You probably answered those questions quickly. When we were children, like our children, we observed and recorded our parents' every move, action, and attitude. We remember minute details that happened years ago.

> *There is nothing concealed that will not be disclosed, or hidden that will not be made known. What you have said in the dark will be heard in the daylight, and what you have whispered in the ear in the inner rooms will be proclaimed from the roofs.*
> —Luke 12:2–3 (NIV)

What do you think your children are recording about you? Let's find out!

FBI Questions:
Uncovering Clues in How You Parent

1. Do you argue frequently with your child's other parent?

2. Do you engage in heated discussions with others in front of your children?

3. Do you badmouth your child's other parent?

4. If you badmouth your child's other parent, does your child become introverted?

5. Do you talk fondly of your child's other parent in the other parent's absence?

6. Do you frequently raise your voice in front of your children?

7. Have you ever brought your child to tears because of the way you were communicating about or to her other parent?

8. Do you think your child is afraid of you?

9. Do you think your child trusts you?

10. Do you think your child trusts his other parent?

11. Does your child confide in you?

12. Does your child confide in her other parent?

13. Are you reliable? Do you do what you promise your child you will do?

14. Are you consistent in the way you treat your child and others?

15. Who do you think your children would say is the person they trust the *most* in their lives? Why?

16. Who do you think your children would say they trust the *least* in their lives? Why?

From the information you just uncovered, do you think your children think you are trustworthy and safe? If you discovered you haven't been trustworthy and safe, would you be willing to go to your children and make amends?

Tough Questions Can Lead to Change

Undoubtedly, you've discovered some surprising or possibly shocking information, so what do you do now?

While answering these FBI Questions, I made painfully disturbing discoveries about myself. I realized that some of my negative behaviors in parenting emulated the same negative behaviors I observed in my father while I was growing up. This is tough to swallow, because I never trusted my father, and I disliked many things about him: his inconsistencies; careless tongue; and flippant temper. I had unconsciously modeled these same negative qualities to my children.

While talking to my friend over a shrimp taco, I sheepishly shared, "You know, I don't think my children trust me as much as they do their father."

She didn't miss a beat, "My kids trust their dad more too."

"Why do people trust each other?" I asked taking another bite of my taco. "Better yet, why did people trust Jesus?"

"He had humility and lived humbly. He treated everyone with the same love and respect. He was consistent and reliable," she piped in. "I would rather have a friend who was reliable and consistent than a friend who always had the answers."

"My research showed clearly that children don't trust their parents when parents dishonor each other through negative attitudes, actions, or words. But I see that my harsh and negative reactions are equally destructive. Taking a step back, I can see how I look through the eyes of my children, and it's not pretty," I said twirling my ice. Susie was quiet.

"I see how their Dad is a steady eddy, and that I have a hair-trigger," I said cautiously. "He carefully crafts his words; I carelessly spew mine."

Susie cupped her mouth with her hands as if she was holding a fire hose to her lips. I giggled.

"Dad gets a handle on things, and I fly off the handle. Dad is even tempered; I am oddly emotional." We both started laughing.

"I don't think we were such bad parents," Susie said trying to console me. "We did the best we could at the time."

"Guess I've got work to do," I said as we paid the bill. We looked at each other, "Hopefully it's not too late."

We get close to those we trust. The more we trust God, the closer we get to Him. The more our children trust us, the closer they get to us.

Driven to the Arms of Grace

I drove away from lunch with Susie feeling sad. When I arrived home, I began processing all that I had discovered and wrote the following thoughts:

> Dear Lord,
> I am weak at this revelation. Is this fixable? I struggle to forgive myself. I am angry at myself for not seeing how my negative patterns affected my children. I mourn because the children I deeply loved—I deeply wounded.

Alone, I fell on my knees and cried to God, "I have failed."
Silence.
"God, I am so frustrated, how can I fix this? Is it repairable?"
Silence.
My body was wracked with pain—pain that I caused. As I picked up my Bible, I felt a warm, gentle touch of a hand in mine. "Is that you Lord?"

I opened the Word and read Psalm 86:5: *"For you, O LORD, are good, and ready to forgive. And abundant in mercy to all those who call upon You."*

He touched my tears and lifted my face. I was taken aback at what I felt—a love so deep, so warm, so pure, so crystal clear I can't look away. "My yoke is easy, my burden is light."

"Let me carry you. I am the way, the truth, and the light. Trust in Me, and I will direct your path. Be still and know that I am God," I heard Him say.

I felt like a newborn kitten cuddling in the warmth and safety of its mother.

"O Lord," I whispered, "You trusted me with these children, and I feel like such a failure. Please forgive me."

"I forgive you, now forgive yourself. Maybe they don't trust you 100 percent, but they've seen you trust Me, and they've learned to trust Me."

I turned to Luke 7: Jesus is talking to Simon about a woman in the city who was a sinner. She knelt at His feet weeping, washed His feet with her tears, and wiped them with her hair. She kissed His feet and anointed them with oil, *"Therefore I say to you, her sins, which are many, are forgiven, for she loved much"* (v. 47).

"I am a sinner, and I do love much. My sins are forgiven? Thank You, Father, that you see my heart for You beats stronger than my sin."

The tears came as grace wrapped His arms around me. There are no perfect parents, only a perfect God who can love and direct imperfect parents.

Forgiven

Even though my children were adults by this time, I knew it wasn't too late to seek forgiveness. I felt if I wanted to begin to build a stronger bond of trust with my children I needed to humble myself and apologize.

As children grow older, they spot our inconsistencies, failures, and, yes, our sins. They notice when we speed on the freeway, gossip about the choir director, gather credit card debt, tell those white lies to avoid driving the carpool, read lust-filled novels, snap at the grocery story clerk, and lie about the toddler's age to get a free ticket on an airline. And the more of the Bible they know, the more easily they spot our moral frailties. You must acknowledge and apologize for your failures.

—Marianne Hering and Jim Weidmann, *The Power of Teachable Moments*

A few days later I called my son and arranged to have lunch with him. As I drove to the restaurant, my stomach began to churn. Why was I nervous? After all, this was my son. I grabbed my purse and headed into the restaurant. We ordered our food and sat at a booth.

"What's up?" he asked.

"I'm working on this chapter about trust, and I'm feeling really convicted; like I haven't been the most trustworthy parent. I feel I have failed you in some areas."

"Mom, what are you talking about?" he said looking at me as if I'd lost my marbles.

"Well I was thinking about all the things I didn't trust about my father, how inconsistent he was, how he was so abrupt and harsh. I hated those things about him."

My son's head was cocked to the side. He was really listening.

"I look at myself and see that I react to you and your sister the same way. I know it's ugly. You know how I can be so impatient, abrupt, and harsh."

"Oh that," he rolled his eyes, he knew exactly what I was talking about. "Mom, maybe you weren't emotionally stable all the time, but you were a good mom."

"Well, I'm sorry; can you forgive me?"

"Sure."

"I love you."

"I love you too."

Just like that, my son graciously forgave me.

Cracking the Code:
Power-Packed Ways to Build Trust

How can parents build trust? By being humble and honest, honoring and respectful, reliable and consistent, just like God. It doesn't matter if your children are 1 or 31.

Think about the character traits of someone you trust. I trust my husband completely. Randy is extremely humble, respectful, honorable, and loving to everybody, not just those who are easy to love. He is also very honest with me about his weaknesses. He has a harder time being honest about his strengths. I reveal my innermost thoughts and feelings to him, because he is consistently reliable and follows through on his word. However, I emotionally isolate myself from those who are arrogant, dishonoring and disrespectful to others, and unreliable and inconsistent.

I have to honestly admit I wish my husband's character traits were as evident in me as they are in him. But I know I fall way short.

• Start with Honesty and Humility

Our children need us to be honest about our weaknesses, struggles, and failures. We cannot project the "perfect persona;" they'll see right through it.

> "My dad never could admit when he did anything wrong. He was a tough and prideful man, and always had all the answers. He is the last person I would go to."
> —Nathan, from an FBI Parent Workshop

Why are we afraid to admit our weaknesses to our children? Tammy Dunahoo, the national director of Foursquare Women, the Foursquare Church, shares this powerful insight:

> "The parents who don't want to admit the good, bad, and ugly about themselves to their children are parents

who most likely are not yet healed from their own woundedness. The insecurity this can cause keeps them putting on the image of what they want their children to believe about them instead of what is true. When children observe parents walking through their own healing process it's amazing what can happen."

I was honest with my son about my weaknesses. And a beautiful thing happened—it didn't drive him away; it drew him closer. When I acknowledged my weaknesses, it made me more approachable. When he observed me walking through the healing process from my painful childhood, it made me more real, more credible. I could see it in the twinkle in his eye, *I know you weren't perfect, Mom, but now I know that you know it too.*

"Children often hear what is not said and these messages tend to speak louder, making a far bigger imprint in them, than words. My children will trust me much more when they know I'm honest about myself, 'Here are my strengths, here are my weaknesses…I know you already see these and you need to know I know they're there too!'"
—Tammy Dunahoo, from a personal interview

• *Respect and Honor Them*
"What are you doing here, Richard?" Karen scowled at her son.
    "I came with Mrs. Jones," Richard said with hurting eyes.
    "Well don't bug me; I'm talking to my friends." She snarled, "Get outside."
    Karen had disrespected her son and embarrassed him in front of her friends. This was a regular pattern, and every time she talked down to him, she pushed him further and further away.
    We dishonor our children by not listening to what they have to say, embarrassing them by talking negatively about them in

front of others, talking down to them, and discouraging them through hurtful words.

How do I honor and respect my friends? I honor them by listening intently to what they have to say, not embarrassing them, and by encouraging them to be all that God has called them to be.

Shouldn't I show my children the same honor and respect I give to my friends?

• *Be Consistent and Reliable*

"My parents would tell us five children that we were going to the movies or skating at night. When night came, they were too tired and changed their minds. 'We'll do it another time.' This was a weekly ritual. After so many years of continual disappointment I learned not to believe them—it hurt too much."

—Richard, from an FBI Parent Workshop

While talking to my son that afternoon, he shared an observation he made about his childhood, "Mom, I know you flipped out and were impatient sometimes, but I have been thinking about how reliable you and Dad were.

"I would go to Charlie's house and one day his dad would let us walk to the store; the next time he was in a bad mood so he wouldn't. It seemed so stupid to me. I always knew that I could walk to the store, I just couldn't cross 82nd. My boundaries didn't change when your mood did, and that was so great."

"Really," I said listening intently. "Maybe I wasn't such a bad mom after all."

"And the whole grounding thing—Mike's mom would be so exasperated with him for talking back that she would scream, 'You're not leaving this house for two weeks,' and then she'd get so tired of him being in the house after two days she'd let up on the grounding. She proved to him that she was a liar. They never followed through on anything; they just screamed a lot. I knew if I smarted back to you or Dad I would be disciplined, and it wasn't such an outrageous consequence. You would take my in-line skates away or make me do the dishes."

Do what you say you are going to do, whether it's taking the kids out for ice cream or disciplining them for talking back.

First Clue Down, Five to Go

Throughout our children's lives we fail them. Throughout our lives our parents failed us. They weren't perfect parents; we aren't perfect parents. Our children won't be perfect parents either.

As my children grew, they discovered that Dad and Mom, as well as siblings, friends, and teachers will let them down. But they also saw their parents go to the One who won't let them down, God. After all, none of us are 100 percent trustworthy, but He is! It's our honor to be able to teach and model that to them.

Great job! You've found your first clue, and discovered the importance of meeting your children's need to trust. Now it's time to move on to clue #2 and remember…you have the right to remain silent as you investigate your children's—and your own—need to be heard.

From the Heart of an Investigator

Remember my conversation with my friend Susie at the beginning of the chapter? We both agreed that we felt our children didn't trust us as much as we would have liked. As I write this, her daughter, Molly, is graduating Saturday from high school; her son Jesse is being deployed to Iraq two days later; another son Joe is leaving for the Czech Republic; her daughter-in-law Brooke is eight days overdue with her first baby; and on Saturday Susie is also supposed to attend the baby shower of another daughter-in-law Jennifer. To say she is in an emotional turmoil is an understatement.

How is she going to get through it? She's going to get through it the same way she has made it through her entire 30 years of parenting: by trusting God, being a trustworthy and reassuring parent, and showing her children that they can trust God too.

"Molly, I know you're scared for your future, but you can do this. God has you in the palm of His hand. He is directing your path."

"Jesse, you are not going alone. We are all going with you; God's going with you. He knew this was coming and trained you for such a time as this. You come from a military family and your grandpas, dad, and uncles are very proud of you. In the Book of Psalms David wrote, *'I will both lie down in peace, and sleep; for you alone, O LORD, make me dwell in safety'* (Psalm 4:8)."

"Brooke, I know you're uncertain of this new baby coming, but God has given you a special love for this child. You are going to be a great mom!"

Because Susie's children hear—and feel—assurance from their mother, it gives them confidence.

Perhaps we shouldn't be so hard on ourselves; maybe we weren't such bad mamas after all.

 Kid's Clue

"When your parents fight, don't blame it on yourself."
—Nequila Truesell, 10
from *Never Eat Anything that Moves*, compiled and illustrated by Robert Bender

CHAPTER 6

Get a Clue #2:

You Have the Right
to Remain Silent

Uncovering your child's
need to be heard

---

*Understand this, my dear brothers and sisters: You must all
be quick to listen, slow to speak, and slow to get angry*
—James 1:19 (NLT)

"One of the most valuable tools an investigator has is
his ears. By skillfully asking questions and listening both
verbally and nonverbally to the answers, he has a greater
chance to solve a mystery."
—Detective Sergeant Dean Hennessey, from a personal
interview

I knew by the vacant look in her sad, brown eyes that she wasn't
listening to me.

"Mommy," I said biting into my cereal, "Are you listening?"

"Huh?" she said as I jolted her from her thoughts.

"Can I go to Lisa's after school?"

No response. "Mom," I said as she slowly exhaled a puff of
smoke from her cigarette.

My eyes followed the grey smoke as it slowly curlicued its way into the air. As it lingered by the kitchen light, I imagined it forming the fancy cursive words: *"Mommy, do you hear me?"*

I was only six years old but I knew her mind was miles away, probably wondering if my dad would come home drunk or sober that night. I put down my spoon, got up, walked over to her, and put my tiny hands on her freshly painted face. Turning her ruby-red-lipstick mouth toward mine, I looked directly into her eyes, "Mommy, are you listening to me?"

"Oh, yes, dear. I'm sorry. I was just thinking about…oh, never mind."

It was really hard to get my mom's full attention with four children, a full-time job, and an alcoholic husband. However, I wasn't competing with my siblings for her attention; I was competing with my mom's faraway thoughts.

After I was grown and had children of my own, I noticed how easy it was for me to drift away to a quieter, more peaceful place, completely tuning out their endless chatter. Often, I would be jolted back to reality by my daughter Heidi's tiny hands as she would cup my freshly made-up face, turn it until our eyelashes touched, and say, "Mommy, are you listening?"

She was doing the same to me as I had done to my mother.

After Heidi was grown and on her own, I went to visit. While we were chatting away, her three-year-old son was trying to get her attention.

"Mommy," he said sweetly.

We kept up our nonstop gab fest.

"Mommy, Mommy," he said growing agitated.

Seeing no response, he gently reached up. With his pudgy hands, he cupped her face and turned her head until they were touching noses. "Mommy, it's my turn to talk."

I started giggling, "You did that to me when you were little." We both laughed, and then I confessed, "I did that to my mother when I was little too."

Listen Up

Based on the more than 1,000 people I interviewed in my research, the need to be heard ranked as the second most important personal need. Unfortunately, for the majority of those people that need went unmet. The resulting pain contributed to why they walked away emotionally, physically, or spiritually from their parents. After documenting hundreds of observations from adult children who didn't feel heard, these four statements kept surfacing again and again:

• "My parents were too busy to listen."

• "My mother wouldn't be quiet long enough for me to get a word in."

• "My dad didn't know how to listen to us kids. He said he was listening, but he wouldn't take his eyes off the television."

• "My parents got mad at me when I shared what I was thinking or feeling, so I stopped talking to them."

Why is it so hard for us to listen? When our children don't feel heard, they don't feel valued, respected, or validated, and they will most likely emotionally, spiritually, or physically shut down. Whoever isn't listening to them will be shut out of their inner thoughts, fears, and dreams. Listening can sometimes seem like a tedious, never-ending task, but have you ever thought about what it will cost if you don't pick up on those clever clues your children are giving you?

I had difficulty listening for two simple reasons: I was too busy talking, and I grew tired of constantly "tuning in" to my children. At other times, I had trouble listening because I was too busy doing mindless tasks, too preoccupied with my own thoughts, or just plain not interested in what my children wanted to talk about. I was a terrible listener, and it cost me dearly, especially in my relationship with my son.

When he was small, my son would try to talk to me, but because I was impatient with him, he grew frustrated and eventually quit trying. Because he didn't feel heard, he shut down, tuned me out, and connected with those who listened to him. Fortunately, one of those he connected with was his father, who, to this day, has an incredibly strong influence on him. It has taken years of keeping my mouth shut and truly listening to what he has to say to repair our relationship. It hasn't been easy. Had I truly believed that silence is golden I would have a richer, deeper relationship with my children today.

> *He who has knowledge spares his words, and a man of understanding is of a calm spirit. Even a fool is counted wise when he holds his peace; when he shuts his lips he is considered perceptive.*
> —Proverbs 17:27–28

Each time I read this Scripture I giggle because it's so simple, yet I fall so short. All I have to do is keep my mouth shut, and I will be counted wise and considered perceptive. Why can't I get this through my head?

FBI Questions:
Uncovering Clues in Your Childhood

1. Who was the easiest person for you to talk to as a child? Why?

2. Who was the hardest person for you talk to as a child? Why?

3. When you were a child, who listened to you and what did the atmosphere around you sound like? *(The car engine noise as your mother listened to you when driving in the car; having Dad to yourself in a quiet house)*

4. When you were a child, who didn't listen to you, and what did the atmosphere around you sound like? *(Dad watching football; Mom's blaring radio)*

5. When you were a child, and someone was listening to you, what were you eating, and what did the atmosphere smell like? *(Special date with Mom having a soda at a local restaurant; cookies at Grandma's house)*

6. When you were a child and someone wasn't listening to you, what were you eating, and what did the atmosphere smell like? *(Stale bread; peanuts from the tavern)*

7. When you were a child and someone was listening to you, what was the expression on his or her face? *(The genuine interest in your grandmother's eyes when you talked to her)*

8. When you were a child and someone wasn't listening to you, what was he or she looking at, and what was the expression on his or her face? *(Dad looking over your shoulder at the television as you tried to talk to him)*

9. When you were a child and someone was listening to you, did he or she gently touch you? How? *(Mother holding your hand when you talked to her; Father with his hand on your back as you hiked in the woods)*

10. Have you discovered something that has brought you pain as you remembered it? What?

11. How can you change the way you think about your past negative experiences?

12. Have you discovered something that has brought you joy as you remembered it? What?

13. How do those experiences affect the way you parent?

14. Who do you think listens to you now?

15. Who do you think doesn't listen to you now?

16. Why do you think that is?

As you undoubtedly just discovered, the people in your life that you were closest to as a child were the people who gave you their undivided attention. They were the parents, grandparents, or friends who gently touched your shoulder, looked into your sparkling eyes, and smiled as you excitedly told them about the frog you almost stepped on. They were the people who made you feel like what you had to say was more important than a special bulletin on the evening news! You probably feel distant from people who ignored you (either consciously or unconsciously), who were so busy talking they didn't listen, or who were just too busy being busy.

Did you solve any valuable mysteries by asking yourself these questions? You may have discovered why you do some of the things you do and can now make the necessary changes to build a stronger relationship with your children.

> "I remind myself every morning; nothing I say this day will teach me anything. So if I'm going to learn, I must do it by listening."
> —Larry King, television talk show host

You Can Tune In

"I had so much to say when I was a child but no one seemed to care," Mary, one of my interviewees, shared introspectively.

"My parents were so busy arguing with each other, screaming at us kids, slamming cupboard doors, and banging pots and pans around in the kitchen, they didn't hear me. Nobody heard me. I shut down. I had the funniest conversations jogging around in my head, but there was no one who wanted to know what they were. Because I never felt heard by my parents, I vowed everyday when I was a child, *When I have children, I'm going to listen to them.*"

Because Mary came from a large, loud family, her voice got lost in the crowd. Day by day, the same message was reiterated, *You're not important; your voice doesn't matter.* Of course they never verbally told her that, but their actions screamed it loud and clear.

"What was your secret for raising such incredible children?" I asked Mary, now a mother of two remarkable boys.

"It was really simple," she said with a quirky little smile, "I listened to them. I never wanted them to feel the pain I felt as a child, because I wasn't heard, wasn't validated."

With a sparkle in her eye she went on, "If you ask them what our family slogan is, they will all say what I have told them all of their lives, 'I will listen to whatever you have to say as long as you talk respectfully to me.'"

Mary—like several hundred other interviewees—needed to be heard. Her parents didn't meet that need, which caused her deep-rooted pain. She ended up connecting with those who did listen to her—her sisters and her peers. When Mary became a parent herself, she could have had clogged ears like her parents, but because of the pain she felt as a child, she was motivated to keep her ears squeaky clean—giving her incredible insight into her children's hearts.

 FBI Questions:
Uncovering Clues in How You Parent

1. Is it easy for your children to talk to you?

2. Do you find it easy to talk to your children?

3. Do you get tired of listening to your children?

4. Do you find your mind wandering when your children are talking?

5. Do you feel you have good communication with your sons?

6. Do you feel you have good communication with your daughters?

7. Do you have the radio on while driving?

8. Do you turn on the television, computer, or stereo the minute you walk in the door?

9. Are your feelings hurt because your son doesn't freely talk to you?

10. Do you feel your daughter talks too much?

11. While your children are talking, are you thinking about what they are saying, or are you thinking about your response to them when they are finished?

12. Do you find yourself interrupting your children when they are speaking?

13. Do you find it difficult to let your children say what they are feeling or thinking?

14. Do you overreact when your children share a thought or feeling that you don't agree with?

15. Do you think your children talk more freely with others than they do to you? If so, why do you think that is?

16. Do you realize that your child's thoughts and feelings are inside them whether they voice them to you or not? Wouldn't you rather have them voice their thoughts and feelings to you than to someone else?

17. What are your children trying to say that you aren't hearing?

18. What does the environment around you sound like when you find it easy to listen?

19. When does the environment around you sound like when you find it hard to listen?

20. What can you do to be a better listener?

21. What new truths have you discovered?

Cracking the Code:
Eight Power-Packed Listening Jewels

Here are eight practical hints to help you as you learn to listen to your children.

• *Listening Jewel #1*
Determine to become a great listener. This listening jewel can be summarized in six simple words: *zip it, zip it, zip it.* Simply shut your mouth. Throughout my life I've discovered that people who talk a lot get tuned out a lot. Boy, did that happen to me. Learn how to turn your voice off and turn your senses on!

• *Listening Jewel #2*
Realize that boys' and girls' listening abilities are different. My friend Diane Davidson always said: Boys want the headlines, and girls want the entire story. My husband totally agrees, "Get to the point, honey." In general, girls are much more verbally communicative than boys—they like details, details, details. I discovered that after about ten words, my son tuned me out. All he heard was: blah, blah, blah. My daughter, on the other hand, wanted to discuss and debate everything.

Author and speaker Rick Johnson writes:

Boys only have about a thirty-second attention span. They literally cannot hear things that don't interest them. Frankly, they don't bother listening most of the time anyway. Some of this short attention span is due to the fact that they focus intently on things that interest them. Part of the problem may be that their minds are somewhere else, and part of it could be that they know Mom will tell them again anyway.
—Rick Johnson, *That's My Son*

• *Listening Jewel #3*
Ask really good questions, and wait patiently for the answers. In silent moments our children have an opportunity to really absorb questions and think about how they really feel about a certain topic.

Nothing more enhances authority than silence. It is the crowning virtue of the strong, the refuge of the weak, the modesty of the proud, the pride of the humble, the prudence of the wise, and the sense of fools.
—Charles de Gaulle, "Of Prestige" (2), *The Edge of the Sword*, 1934, tr. Gerald Hopkins, 1960

• *Listening Jewel #4*
If possible, talk in quiet, distraction-free places. My son opened up to me while driving in the car. My daughter felt comfortable to talk at night while I tucked her in bed. Other ideas: take walks or hikes; swing at the park; get a soda at their favorite restaurant.

• *Listening Jewel #5*
Remember, timing is everything; it's easiest to listen when you're not tired, stressed, or hungry!

• *Listening Jewel #6*
Don't instantly react when your child is sharing something that you don't agree with. Try to remain calm and see the heart behind what they are trying to say.

Linda, one of the parents I've coached, shared, "When my four sons became teenagers, I realized I was afraid to let them talk, to tell me what they were thinking or feeling, because I didn't like what they were saying. The choices they were making and the things they were interested in made me nervous. One day I was sharing my frustration with my friend, and she said something profound: 'Linda, don't you realize that even if you don't let them talk to you about their thoughts and feelings, those same thoughts and feelings are still inside of them. They will get it out one way or the other, either through behavior or through talking it out with friends—someone who isn't threatening, and someone who will listen.'"

• *Listening Jewel #7*
Don't expect to have deep conversations with your children at the grocery store, at a skating rink, at a video arcade, or on your way to church. And don't expect them to talk when they're with a group of their friends. I have tried all of these situations and can tell you it doesn't usually work.

When you want to have a meaningful extended conversation, use some investigative thought and planning and take your child on a Daddy or Mommy date. Choose to keep your mouth closed, and let your child talk freely and uninterrupted.

My son takes his 3-year-old son, Isaiah, on a Daddy date, usually to the park or someplace to eat. He does the same on another day with his 5-year-old daughter, Trinity, but usually they go to the mall. He also has found a way to connect to his 15-year-old sister-in-law, whom he and his wife have custody of: he takes her shopping as well.

You'll find if you let your children lead the conversations as you follow them around, the fun really begins. Think of these times as mystery dates, opportunities to discover something new.

• *Listening Jewel #8*

Concentrate on what your child is saying not on what you want to say when he or she is finished talking. Don't you just hate it when you are trying to talk with somebody and they keep interrupting? I'm guilty, guilty, guilty as charged. Or what about when, the minute you stop talking, they spit out something that has nothing to do with what you were talking about? I've done that too, and it's hurtful, disrespectful, and impolite.

> "The deepest rivers flow with the least sound."
> —Quintus Curtius Rufus, first century A.D.

It's Worth It

Every parent can learn to become a better listener. It is a skill worth perfecting. Your children will thank you for it.

Good job! You've now uncovered the first two clues: your children's need to trust, and your children's need to be heard. You're almost half way there. Now it's time to discover the treasures that come with clue #3: your child's need to be valued and to understand true value. See if you can find any hidden secrets!

From the Heart of an Investigator

"Lori, you talk too much!" said Betty Mitchell, my counselor training coach. "You are missing so much that God has for you, because you're so busy talking you aren't listening. You need to learn to be quiet."

I was stunned; I was embarrassed, and I was angry. *That can't be true,* I reasoned to myself, but deep down I knew it was. The reality was my mouth was constantly on the run, and someone had abruptly tripped me and it hurt. Staggering from her office I thought back through my life. I saw how my words had alienated friends, coworkers, my husband, and my children. But I was still in denial at how much damage my lack of listening had caused.

I'll show her, I thought. For two weeks I practiced being quiet, and—ouch!—did it hurt. My flesh wanted to let 'er rip—let my words frolic freely—but my spirit was drawn to tone down, tune in, hear, see, and experience the beautiful mysteries Betty said were eluding me. Mysteries God wanted to reveal to me.

As I zipped my lips and kept my mouth from flapping, she was absolutely right: magnificent mysteries began to unfold. My little world became a peaceful, brighter place. My ears perked up at the sound of the sweet chirping of robins outside my kitchen window. My husband's green eyes radiated a joy I hadn't been aware of. My friends became smarter. And most important, my children began to open up to me like red rose buds in spring—well, maybe I'm exaggerating that a bit, but I did notice their smiles appeared whiter and brighter, their eyes radiated peace, and their infectious giggles swallowed me up in joy. How could I have been missing this?

"Mom, you've got to see this," Nicholas said excitedly as he pulled me toward his computer. "I got the best deal on these three microphones off eBay."

"Mom, listen to this song," Heidi said modestly. "I wrote it last week when I was feeling sad."

I'm still working on keeping my mouth shut and my ears open, but with God's help I am beginning to see the value of listening.

 Kid's Clue

"My baby brother, Nathan, cries all the time, because he doesn't want to be a baby."
—Joshua Goddard, 5, my grandson

CHAPTER 7

Get a Clue #3:

Investigating Value

Uncovering your child's
need to be valued and to
understand true value

"Look at the birds. They don't plant or harvest or store food in barns, for your heavenly Father feeds them. And aren't you far more valuable to him than they are?"
—Matthew 6:26 (NLT)

At every turn, they [young people] are bombarded with hedonistic, self-gratifying messages. Day in and day out, they are bombarded with the message that life is all about toys and pleasures and satisfying every hormonal urge.
—Charles Colson and Nancy Pearcey, *How Now Shall We Live?*

Investigators, like parents, make many disturbing discoveries in their journey. In my three-year investigation, I made a disturbing, though obvious, discovery: parents have bought into the deception that if their children have all the latest toys, electronic gadgets, French manicures, and designer clothes, not to mention straight As and first place in the track meet, they will be happier, and feel more important, more valued. We are teaching our children that they are valuable because of what they have, how they perform, and how they look, not because of who they are. But who they are is what truly matters: children of the Most High God, made in His image for His glory.

Sadly, through well-meaning parents and friends, and maybe not-so-well-meaning television shows, movies, commercials, and music, our children are being hammered with a relentless flood of deceptive messages, *Get bigger, get shinier, get better, get faster, get newer, get the most expensive. Be the best, be the prettiest, be the smartest, jump the highest, run the fastest. And if you do, then you're somebody, you're valuable.* Everywhere they look, our children see affluence and success as power, and they misinterpret this power as value.

The outcome of this misconception is costly. Through interviews and FBI Parenting Workshops I have met many parents and children who, unfortunately, discovered this delusion too late.

From Fake Beauty to Real Ashes

Brenda thought she had it all. In fact she thought she was it all!

A hush fell in the quaint little chapel. One by one heads turned as 22-year-old Brenda strolled into the room. It was as if she were walking the red carpet into a Hollywood premiere, the spotlight directly on her. With her movie-star good looks— golden-weaved hair, sun-bronzed sculptured body, and fire-engine-red lips—she was obviously aware of the effect her grand entrance made on everyone in the room. All eyes were on her. She reeked of money, lots of money.

As she brushed by my chair I noticed her beautiful hands with impeccably manicured nails. Her appearance struck me as odd because we were in a drug and alcohol rehabilitation center where I was teaching an FBI Parenting Workshop. I thought, *How could she get her nails done in here?* She looked extremely out of place in her pink stilettos and white leather jacket.

The contrast was like oil and water. She sat next to a plainly dressed girl who looked like she had just rolled out of bed: messed up hair, wrinkled clothes, no makeup. In fact, all the other girls in the room looked like they had just rolled out of bed.

I listened as Brenda told how her financially well-off parents raised her in a deeply religious, Christian home. Her father worked on the road and was rarely home. She never had to work for anything and was given anything she wanted.

Her family dubbed her "the mad princess." They showered her with adoration, gifts, the latest designer clothes, and money. Ever since she was a little girl she had been pampered and received attention, because she was beautiful. Brenda began to think her value was tied to her looks and her family's wealth. As she grew older, she came to need the adoration and praise of others and often received it for her looks or possessions. After all, if she got attention, she was "somebody." Her identity and self-worth were in what she had, how she looked or performed, instead of who she was: a child of God made for His purpose.

As she grew older she became increasingly dissatisfied with herself. She never thought she looked good enough or had enough. She found her fulfillment fleeting. She went through friends like tissue, using them a little and then throwing them away. She reasoned that they were jealous of her. Boyfriends? Wow, did she have gorgeous boyfriends. But she was always looking over her shoulder for someone cuter, smarter, or more athletic. She started going to parties, where she was introduced to drugs, which catapulted her into a dark, dark world. Never realizing that what she was looking for didn't exist, she was hoping her outer world would bring her the joy that can only be attained through knowing God and discovering the inner beauty and purpose He'd given her.

Unfortunately for Brenda, her entire foundation was built on superficiality, even though her parents loved her dearly, lived with godly principles, and wanted nothing but the best for her. She didn't understand that her true beauty would radiate from her heart.

*Do not let your adornment be merely outward—arranging
the hair, wearing gold, or putting on fine apparel—rather let
it be the hidden person of the heart, with the incorruptible
beauty of a gentle and quiet spirit, which is very precious in
the sight of God.*
—1 Peter 3:3–4

Genuine Beauty Revealed!

"Brenda, why did you believe you were valuable as a child?"
I asked.

She seemed baffled. "I honestly don't know," she said in her
southern drawl. "I remember my parents telling me I was so cute
and their little princess."

"Did anyone ever tell you that you are valuable because
you're a child of God? He made you unique. You are extremely
valuable, just because you're His kid. You don't have to look a
certain way, act a certain way, or be perfect. He loves you just the
way you are. He made you in His image. He gave you beautiful
gifts that are inside of you, that He wants to use for His glory."

Brenda's eyes softened, a sweet smirk spread across her face.
I could tell she was considering what I said.

"Well, I never thought about that," she looked up out of the
corners of her eyes. "I guess I was too busy trying to be cute."

She paused, "My parents drove a Mercedes. We lived in a
great neighborhood. I always felt like I had to get straight As, be
the best at everything. I guess I grew up believing I was better
than others if I looked pretty and was the best at what I did. If
I felt pretty and smart and got attention, I guess I was important,
I was valuable."

We both got quiet. "I don't have to be perfect? I don't have to
be the best?" Her thoughts came out as a game of verbal Ping-Pong.
"I'm special just because I'm God's child? Hmm, I don't know about
that. All my life I thought I was special because I was cute, and I
guess that doesn't matter to God or anyone else does it?"

During the next several months I watched as Brenda began
to travel a new road, one that took her on a journey to nurture

and cultivate the beauty that sat dormant inside of her. The focus of her life went from getting love and attention to discovering her God-given gifts. By discovering these gifts, she learned to give love, instead of expect love and attention from others.

As she began to know God through the Bible, Brenda made precious discoveries about why she is valuable. Now she is teaching these to her young daughter:

> For you formed my inward parts; You covered me in my mother's womb.
>
> I will praise You, for I am fearfully and wonderfully made; Marvelous are Your works, and that my soul knows very well.
>
> My frame was not hidden from You, when I was made in secret, and skillfully wrought in the lowest parts of the earth. Your eyes saw my substance, being yet unformed. And in Your book they all were written, the days fashioned for me, when as yet there were none of them.
>
> How precious also are Your thoughts to me, O God! How great is the sum of them!
> —Psalm 139:13–17

As the truth of God's Word saturated her mind and heart, the bright lights and loud voice of the world faded. Brenda transformed from a selfish, self-centered brat to a radiant, bright-eyed, purpose-filled child of God. She discovered how giving to others gave her life deep, eternal, purposeful value, something that the elusive "getting" had tried to rob from her. The "mad princess" became the "peace-filled princess."

What Are You Investing In?

How do I know if I'm properly teaching my children why they are valuable? Teaching our children why they are valuable is like walking a tight rope. If we shower them with constant praise and adoration, because of their accomplishments, outward appearance, and material possessions, they become self-focused, self-obsessed, and develop a "sense of entitlement." However, if we don't encourage or praise them at all they may think they are of no worth, causing deep feelings of insecurity. Throughout my investigation I have seen both extremes and have seen the devastation both caused. Neither is pretty; both are disturbing. The key is to find balance. So how do we discover the correct balance?

The answer lies in knowing our children individually and in knowing ourselves. It just doesn't happen. We have to think about what our lives are saying. The most effective way our children learn from us is through observing our behavior. What are our choices and behaviors teaching our children?

While growing up, Brenda's parents invested in what they thought was valuable: ballet lessons, expensive clothes, private schools, new cars, and gadgets. By concentrating on her looks and her performance, her parents naively encouraged her to develop an obsessive focus on herself. They invested their time and money in what they valued: her outward beauty and accomplishments. Unfortunately they didn't invest in helping her develop virtues such as integrity, honesty, charity, reliability, and compassion. Jesus said, *"For where your treasure is, there your heart will be also"* (Matthew 6:21). Chances are, where your treasure is your child's treasure will be also.

FBI Questions
Let's investigate where you invest your time!

1. How many hours a day do you spend:
   - Working at a job or around the house _____
   - Taking children to dance, soccer, volleyball lessons _____
   - Shopping, hobbies, Internet, watching TV_____
   - Going to the gym, primping _____
   - Quiet time, Bible study, church activities _____
   - Praying for others_____
   - Helping children reach out to others _____

2. How many hours a day do you spend on relationships:
   - Time with spouse _____
   - Time with friends _____
   - Time with other family _____
   - Time with co-workers _____
   - Time with first child _____
   - Time with second child _____
   - Time with third child _____
   - Time with fourth child _____
   - Time with fifth child _____
   - Time with sixth child _____

3. Where do you spend the majority of your time?

4. Where would your spouse say you spend most of your time?

5. Where would your children say you spend most of your time?

6. What would your children say you spend most of your time talking about?

7. Do you provide opportunities for your children to give time to others?

8. Do your children see you living honestly, charitably, and compassionately?

9. What would you like to change about the way you spend your time?

10. Have you discovered anything new that you weren't aware of?

Let's investigate where you invest your money!

11. How much money a month do you spend on:
   - Lessons for children _____

- Shopping for children _____
- Shopping for yourself _____
- Entertainment: sports, movies, theater _____
- Giving food, clothes, or money to the homeless or those less fortunate _____
- Tithes, offerings, missions projects _____

12. What is where you spend your money telling your children?

13. Do you talk to your children about why you are giving to the church, to the homeless, or to missions?

14. Do you provide opportunities for your children to give financially to others?

Let's investigate how much you value accomplishments!

15. Do you feel you have to be better than everyone else at what you do?

16. Do you ever make your children feel guilty for getting less than perfect grades?

17. Do you ever make remarks like, "You could lose the weight if you wanted to?"

18. Do you praise your children if they make a soccer goal, yet scream at them or ignore them if they don't?

19. Do you praise your child when they stick up for children who are being picked on?

20. Do you lovingly teach your children that a good attitude when they don't win is more valuable than actually winning?

Honestly...

If you answered these questions honestly, you discovered that the truth can be brutal. However, before you slam this book shut or throw it against the wall, be courageous, and remember in your honest answers lie the clues to your child's heart. The answers reveal things about you and what you think is valuable. What did you discover you're investing in?

One Last Question

What did Jesus invest in?

Did He (or His disciples) invest in the shiniest new electronic, super-high-tech fishing gadgets? Did He invest in building a fishing fleet or a prominent name and empire? No! No! Jesus didn't value extravagant castles, impressive royal gowns, crowns, or jewels. He didn't invest in making His name prestigious, in gaining worldwide fame, vast fortunes, or high-status friends. He invested in what God had called Him to do, spreading God's love through relationships—relationships with people and a relationship with God. He invested time teaching, training, serving, and loving His 12 disciples and many others. And He valued spending time alone with God. He invested in what He valued and that was you, me, and our children. *"But when He saw the multitudes, He was moved with compassion for them, because they were weary and scattered, like sheep having no shepherd"* (Matthew 9:36).

Don't Conform

OK, so perhaps you've discovered that you have been investing your time and money focusing on superficial things. What do you do now? Feel guilty? Feel condemned? Feel bad for yourself? No, change your focus. When we change our focus, we can change our behavior.

Look what the Lord said to Samuel: *"Do not look at his appearance or at his physical stature, because I have refused him. For the LORD does not see as man sees; for man looks at the outward appearance, but the LORD looks at the heart"* (1 Samuel 16:7).

The Lord told Samuel to change his focus, quit looking at the outward appearance and focus on the heart.

So how do we change our focus? Romans 12:2 says, *"Do not be conformed to this world, but be transformed by the renewing of your mind."* But what does that mean? Renewing means revitalizing our thoughts, refocusing on what truly is important, meditating, contemplating, and pondering the truth of God's Word. Through the power of the Holy Spirit, we can read the Word of God, and it will change us from the inside out.

> *Finally, brethren, whatever things are true, whatever things are noble, whatever things are just, whatever things are pure, whatever things are lovely, whatever things are of good report, if there is any virtue and if there is anything praiseworthy—meditate on these things. The things which you learned and received and heard and saw in me, these do, and the God of peace will be with you.*
> —Philippians 4:8–9

Notice this Scripture doesn't tell us to think about whatever things are pretty, whatever things are expensive, whatever things are shiny, whatever things are the best, whoever is the smartest, whoever is the best athlete, whoever has the best body, whoever has the most toys, or whoever has the best grades. And my twist on verse nine would be: If you focus and accept those things which you learn and receive and hear and see in the world, undoubtedly you will live in a state of confusion and inadequacy and fear will be with you. It sounds preposterous that anyone would choose to live this way, but that's exactly what is happening around us (and sometimes to us) on a daily basis.

Through workshops and coaching, I have witnessed parents like Brenda's make a 180-degree turn once the reality of what they have been focusing on and investing in comes to light. Later, Brenda told me her parents were repulsed when they realized that their focus had been on performance, accomplishments, and material possessions. They hadn't seen it. By changing their investments and focus from outward things—performance, possessions and physical beauty—to inner virtues—honesty, integrity, charity, reliability and compassion—they, along with Brenda, discovered true, God-given value.

OK, now we've covered the importance of teaching our children why they are valuable—because they're made in God's image. And we've looked at what we spend our time, money, and thoughts on. Now comes the third and final step: identifying ways we can make our children feel valued!

Failing to Connect

How do we know when other people value us? They spend time with us. They talk to us with respect. They listen to us. They validate what we say. Their eyes light up, and they seem delighted when we walk into a room. They are genuinely happy to be with us. Their words and their body language convey, *You are valuable, you are loved, just for being you.*

In my three-year investigation, I interviewed numerous adult children who had been in serious trouble. I asked them if they felt valued growing up and by whom. Many young men shared that they didn't feel valued by their fathers, because the fathers were absent, either through divorce or abandonment. But what shocked me was that many of the men interviewed told me their fathers did live with them, but these fathers often chose to be emotionally or physically absent. While living in the same home, they failed to make a lasting connection with their children.

Jack loved and admired his father, Steve. Steve gave his son everything except what Jack needed most: his time. Feeling guilty because he was often out of town working, Steve, when he was home, showered his son with roller blades, expensive hockey gear, and CDs—anything Jack asked for. Unfortunately, Steve conveyed to his son, "Your wish is my command." He reasoned, *I value and love my son so much I am going to give him all the things my father never gave me.*

When Jack was young he constantly pleaded with his dad: "Daddy do you have to leave?; let's go play catch." "Daddy, please can we go fishing?" After years of unheeded pleas, he quit voicing his need and internalized this thought, *If I were valuable, Dad would want to spend time with me. I must not be worth much.*

Jack emotionally drifted from his father, daily harboring pain, which turned to anger. He began getting in trouble in school, at church, and eventually winding up in jail. When he disconnected from his father, he began connecting with friends, embracing their habits and views of life.

Both father and son had different definitions of what was valuable. Steve placed value on providing his son with material things. Jack's definition of value was spending time with his father. Their values clashed, costing Steve a strong bond with his son. Because the father didn't understand his son's need to be valued through time and not material possessions, both father and son lost.

FBI Questions:
Uncovering Clues in Your Childhood

Let's discover what and who made you feel valued as a child.

1. When you were a child, what did it sound like when you felt valued? *(Mom telling you a bedtime story; laughing together; "Wow, what a big fish you caught! Good job.")*

2. When you were a child, what did being devalued sound like? *(Dad telling you to shut up; "Why don't you ever think?"; yelling; fighting; broken promises; name calling)*

3. When you were a child, what did being valued feel like to you? *(Hugs; cuddles; good eye contact; kisses on the cheek; sitting on Dad's lap; tickling; scratching your back)*

4. When you were a child, what did being devalued feel like? *(Being slapped, flicked, or yelled at; being kicked in the rear)*

5. When you were a child, when you felt valued, what did it taste like? *(Fresh cookies at Grandma's house; a favorite meal; Dad making French toast)*

6. When you were a child, what did being devalued taste like? *(Burnt macaroni and cheese; overcooked or dried up food left on the kitchen counter)*

7. When you were a child, when you felt valued, what did it smell like? *(Grandpa's aftershave; clean sheets; cookies baking; bacon frying)*

8. When you were a child, when you felt devalued, what did it smell like? *(Dad's stale beer breath; Mom's cigarettes)*

9. When you were a child, when you felt valued, what did it look like to you? *(Sharing a family movie; seeing Mom spend time with God; baking cookies; smiling)*

10. When you were a child, what did feeling devalued look like? *(Being left alone at home; Mom giving you a disgusted look; parents' vacant stares as you tried to talk to them)*

Investigating Not Prosecuting

Undoubtedly, you just recalled some memories that have long been buried. Some may be pleasant, others not so. You may be experiencing joy at remembering heartwarming moments or perhaps shame and embarrassment, maybe deep hurt or lingering unforgiveness. As I have taught workshops, this session often proves to be highly emotional.

Remember chapter 2—we're not seeking someone to blame, we're seeking the truth. Facing the pain will lead to resolve; resolve leads to change; and change empowers you! We're looking at how we were treated as children to see if we are parenting our children in similar ways. If we need to change, we can change.

FBI Questions:
Uncovering Clues in How You Parent

Now let's answer the same questions from your child's point of view.

1. What do you think feeling valued sounds like to your children? *("Wow, honey you look great!" "Thanks for going to the store with me.")*

2. What do you think feeling devalued sounds like to your children? *("Quit bothering me." "Stop crying." "I'll give you something to cry about.")*

3. What does being valued feel like to your children? *(Hugs, cuddles, eye contact, arm around the shoulder)*

4. What does being devalued feel like to your children? *(Pushing them away when they want to cuddle)*

5. What does feeling valued taste like to your children? *(Ice cream at the parlor; a date at their special restaurant; fresh cookies)*

6. What does feeling devalued taste like to your children? *(Burnt macaroni and cheese; cold hot dogs)*

7. What does feeling valued smell like to your children? *(Roses, chocolate, special cologne, eggs on Saturday morning)*

8. What do you think devalued smells like to your children? *(Stale beer, cigarette smoke)*

9. What do you think value looks like to your children? *(Shopping, skiing, or biking together; showing up at their games; having special dates with just them)*

10. What do you think devalued looks like to your children? *(Children waiting in the car while you talk nonstop to your friend)*

11. Have you discovered anything that has surprised you? Have you discovered areas you would like to change?

Let's Keep Going!

Do you feel like you've just been interrogated? Remember, my goal is to help you gain an eye-opening perspective of how life looks through your children's eyes, not to make you feel guilty. We are investigating, not prosecuting!

Perhaps these questions helped you uncover negative behaviors, targeting problem areas you didn't know were there. Maybe you haven't been making your child feel valued or you have been valuing them for the wrong reasons; maybe you have been de-valuing your child and you didn't even know it. Perhaps you've discovered you're displaying some of the same negative behaviors with your children that your parents did with you. Whatever you discovered, hurrah! Now you can do something about it. You can change.

How Do I Change?

When I discover disturbing things in the way I parent, I go to God in prayer. I ask Him for forgiveness. I pray for the strength to change. I pray that He will restore my relationships with my children to His original design. And I continue to ask these things on a daily basis. As I've said before, and as my children will attest, I am far from perfect and am in profound need of grace. It's magnificent when you receive grace from God and then from your children.

Many times through the years, I have packed up my pesky pride, strapped on humility, and humbly approached my children to apologize for my devaluing reactions and responses, my outbursts of anger, and most often, the hurtful things I've said to them. Do my children make nasty remarks and walk away? No, quite the opposite, they graciously accept my apology and lovingly forgive me. By doing that, I've become real and approachable to them.

Are you open to asking God for forgiveness? Can you ask God to give you the strength and humility to talk openly and honestly with your children about what you've discovered? Are you open to acknowledging your failures with your children? Are you open to asking them for forgiveness for your devaluing responses and reactions?

Cracking the Code: Love Languages

You have uncovered some interesting findings in this chapter: the importance of teaching your child why they are valuable and understanding what makes your child feel valued. In my years of parenting and coaching, one of the best books I've found about connecting with children is *The Five Love Languages of Children* by Gary Chapman and Ross Campbell, MD. In his book he shares five ways people feel valued and loved: physical touch, words of affirmation, quality time, acts of service, and gifts. Here's the practical application. You need to use your investigative senses and sniff out your children's primary love language and then show them they're valued in the appropriate way. (And it wouldn't hurt to figure out your own love language and your spouse's too).

Can you guess your child's primary love language? Do they like hugs? Do they like encouraging and affirming words? Do they like to spend quality time with you? Do they like presents? Do they like when you do things for them? It's important to know what their individual love language is so you can express your love for them in the most meaningful way. My daughter, for example, loves gifts; her eyes light up at the sight of a gift bag. My son, on the other hand, gets excited when I spend quality time with him. If I shower him with gifts, it means nothing. What does your child need from you to feel valued?

On to Clue #4

Congrats! You have once again tromped through the trenches and bravely and courageously faced the truth. You've uncovered clue #1:

your children's need to trust; clue #2: their need to be heard; and clue #3: their need to be valued and understand why they are valuable. As an efficient special agent you get to advance to clue #4. This is your mission if you choose to accept it: put on your spy glasses as you uncover your children's need for purpose not pampering.

From the Heart of an Investigator

As a child I struggled to understand my value. Unlike Brenda, I often felt embarrassed at my upbringing.

When I was in the seventh grade I lived in the oldest run-down house in the neighborhood. Broken cars littered the mud driveway (everyone else's was paved). Overgrown grass, dirty porch. One afternoon I was standing in the mud yard. Suddenly I heard, "Beep, beep." I looked up and saw Jake from my junior high school, hanging out of his parents' shiny new blue 1969 Ford Mustang. "Hey, Laura," he yelled and waved as the car sped past.

My heart began to pound; my face grew hot. I froze. I felt like I was in slow motion. *Should I wave? Will I look stupid?* And then he was gone. Embarrassed, I ran up the steps into my house. I fell on the bed, burying my head in the pillow.

"Oh no, oh no, oh no," I screamed. "My little secret's out. Now everyone will know what a dump I live in." I began praying over and over, "Dear God, don't let him tell anyone! Please, don't let him tell anyone!"

The next morning I reluctantly got ready for school. I loathed the thought of running into Jake. Walking to the bus stop I whispered, "Dear God, don't let me run into him at school."

All day I nervously crept from class to class, hoping to avoid Jake. "Class dismissed!" my teacher exclaimed.

Whew, I made it, I thought. *I never bumped into him once all day.*

The bell rang. I shyly poked my head out the door before slipping down the hall. *I'm almost home free,* I snickered to myself.

Bam. I heard a locker slam behind me. I looked up and there he stood—the monster I had dreaded seeing all day—Jake "Preppy" Jones. His eyes glared, an evil smile broke out across his face, and his megaphone voice boomed, "Hey Laura, was that your dump you were standing out in front of yesterday?"

I was mortified. My ghastly white face grew red hot. I looked at the speckled floor, tears streaming down my face, dripping from my nose. I swished my long blonde hair in front of my eyes, closing a curtain to my wounded soul. As I slithered down the hall, I blindly made my way to the bus.

I never told anyone, except my grandma Grina. She knew Jake's grandma and bought flowers at her business. As tears pooled in her eyes she told me, "I will never step foot in their business again." And she didn't.

It was only several years later that I came to know my value wasn't in what I wore or where I lived. My value was in being a child of God, deeply loved by Him. He had given me virtuous gifts that He wanted me to use to bless the lives of others: compassion, empathy, humility, charity, kindness, and more.

However, as a junior high kid I didn't know that. I truly wish my parents, throughout my young life, would have reinforced to me why I was valuable: I am a child of God who is called according to His purpose.

I challenge you to look everyday for opportunities to teach your children about why their lives are valuable: they were made for a special purpose. And teach them to use that understanding to reach out and value others.

Kid's Clue

"In a perfect world my mom wouldn't be so weird and wave to people she doesn't know."
—Melissa Murray, 12
from *Lima Beans Would Be Illegal*, compiled and illustrated by Robert Bender

CHAPTER 8

Get a Clue #4:

This Is Your Mission
If You Choose to Accept It

Uncovering your child's need
to have purpose not pampering

*God has given each of you some special abilities; be sure to
use them to help each other, passing on to others God's many
kinds of blessings.*
—1 Peter 4:10 (TLB)

If you ask any forensic scientist, detective, investigator, or
police officer to describe the difficult aspects of their job, they
could bark out their answers faster than a dog buries a bone:
time consuming; sometimes boring; emotionally draining;
discouraging; messy, smelly, and gory; constant interruptions;
long hours. Sounds a lot like parenting.

However, when asked why they do it, many would reply,
"I believe I am doing something that will make a difference,
possibly make the world a better place." Purpose. Their jobs
give them a sense of accomplishment, a sense of value. And they
experience fulfillment.

Training, managing, and performing with hundreds of children
for more than seven years as director of The Bee-Bop Kids,

I saw children embrace a deep sense of purpose at incredibly young ages, giving them rich compassion for others, a sense of accomplishment, and a sense of value. They experienced fulfillment.

Changed by Rio

The Bee-Bop Kids did evangelistic outreach using singing, dancing, and drama. We were invited to tour and minister in Brazil, and I was shocked that 24 brave and loving parents of grade-school and junior-high kids said yes. After several months of training, with 6 chaperones and 12 children ages 10 to 14, we excitedly set off on a 21-day ministry tour of eight of the biggest cities in Brazil. Our first stop: the crime capital of the world, Rio de Janeiro. Our family had been to Brazil a few times and had housed 8 exchange students from Rio, so we were quite familiar with the intense crime and drug problems. The members of our team, however, were about to receive the education of their lives.

As our bus rattled through the crowded streets, we noticed young, filthy, raggedly dressed children swarming in a park we were passing. "Slow down, slow down!" I yelled to the bus driver. Noticing their strange behavior, I turned and whispered to one of our leaders, "Those children look like vultures getting ready to attack something. Are they scoping out victims?"

Gawking out the mud-caked bus window, I spotted a little boy with brown tear-stained cheeks, about eight years old, helping another little boy, about five, do something. I squinted—face pressed to the window—to get a better look. "What are they doing? They're doing something with a red paper bag." I looked around, noticing several other street kids with puffed out little red bags. As the tiny boy bent his head down into the bag, I noticed his filthy, matted dark brown hair. I tried to get a closer look.

The kids on the other side of the bus jumped over to our side and pressed their faces to the window. "He's sniffing glue," our Brazilian leader said nonchalantly. "The older boy is teaching the younger how to do it." I felt sick to my stomach. These were just babies.

He explained, "Those cute little children are addicted to glue and mug whoever travels through this park. They travel in packs and are anything but sweet and innocent. They're like animals."

As we solemnly drove through the dirty streets, it started to rain. Arriving back at our lush hotel in downtown Copacabana, we jumped out of the bus, escorted by hotel security guards, and were ushered into the gated building. Once inside the warm, dry building, the kids ran up the steps toward the restaurant. They heard some commotion outside and jetted toward the window. Outside on the dark, cold, wet sidewalk, were six or seven young children that looked to be ages 4 to 12. A few of the girls from our group stayed with me at the window and observed with curiosity. We were shocked as we watched them furiously pull each other's hair, hit, scratch, and scream at each other.

"What are they fighting about?" Allysen asked. We observed a little longer. "They're fighting for a dry spot under the overhang of the building," I said quietly. The rain began to pound, saturating the children below. *They look like wild, drowned cats,* I thought. Just then a little girl glanced up at the window and shot us a vicious look. But her sullen eyes, shredded dirty jeans, sopping wet hair, and mud-stained face seemed to be pleading with me.

"She's looking at us: we have to do something," whimpered Corinna.

"They look so miserable," added Jennifer.

There was a cold silence. "They're just little kids!" Heidi said as a tear slid down her face.

"Why are they out there and we're in here?" Christy cried, tears flowing freely down her face, like the rain relentlessly streaming down the window.

Once the homeless children figured out their pecking order, they lay down on their soaking wet cardboard, lining up their little bodies like puppies suckling their mom, heads tucked against the building, legs sticking out in the rain. But, they weren't cuddling with a warm mama; they were lying blanketless. Curled into the fetal position, they shivered, struggling to get comfortable on the cold, hard, wet cement.

One by one our girls put their arms around each other. Gathered in a huddle, they cried. "It's not fair. Why are they out there and we're in here?"

"Some of those kids are younger than we are. Where are their parents?" Their cries turned to uncontrollable sobs. They began to pray, "Dear God, we don't understand this. Those kids are our age, and it's not fair. Why don't You do something for them?"

God's Word Became Real to Them

As leaders, we tried to console our children, but deep down we knew God was doing a far greater work.

They were experiencing something Paul writes about in Romans. *"The Spirit Himself bears witness with our spirit that we are children of God, and if children, then heirs—heirs of God and joint heirs with Christ, if indeed we suffer with Him, that we may also be glorified together"* (Romans 8:16–17, emphasis added).

They were suffering with Christ. They were touching the heart and pain of God. He was using this cold, dreary night to let these bright, privileged, American girls feel His broken heart, and the deep pain He has for His children. And in the midst of intense pain, He birthed a lifelong compassion and empathy in our children for others.

I thank God for allowing our children to experience His heartache on the first day of our trip to Rio. Over the next three weeks that pain fueled the hearts of our kids as they poured out God's love, being His arms, His smile, His hope, His joy, His peace, His kindness, to several thousand children.

They also experienced another life-changing truth that one day earlier had just been a story in the Bible. *"Religion that God our Father accepts as pure and faultless is this: to look after orphans and widows in their distress and to keep oneself from being polluted by the world"* (James 1:27 NIV).

What happens to the lives of children when they are exposed to the painful circumstances other children are born into? Does it hurt them? Do they become fearful? No, actually the opposite happens. Having led many missions trips involving children, I have been privileged to witness children metamorphose from self-obsessed, ungrateful children into caring human beings with a deep sense of purpose, compassion, and gratefulness in a matter of weeks.

Does it have to be a foreign missions trip? Absolutely not! There are obvious needs all around us: we just need to see them and help our children see them. Children who are exposed to others' needs and sufferings and allowed to help—feeding their local homeless, taking food to an elderly neighbor, handing out care packages at a freeway off-ramp—are blessed. By serving others they experience, at a very young age, both humility and mercy. *"He has shown you, O man, what is good; and what does the LORD require of you but to do justly, to love mercy, and to walk humbly with your God?"* (Micah 6:8).

They also learn that they have something to offer that relieves the pain of others. *"God has given each of you some special abilities; be sure to use them to help each other, passing on to others God's many kinds of blessings"* (1 Peter 4:10 TLB).

Where are they now? The Bee-Bop Kids are grown now except for Allysen Croeni, who died of cancer a few years after this trip. However, her missions-minded legacy lives on in her parents and other missions-minded teens. We all miss her.

Many of The Bee-Bop Kids continue to lead lives of service. Rachel lived in Romania, working with abandoned children, then taught school in Uzbekistan, and currently lives in the United States working for Habitat for Humanity. Katie became Miss America in 2002 and speaks nationally raising awareness for breast cancer. Shelly is in full-time children's and marriage ministry. Joanna helps in a college outreach at Radford University in Virginia and leads a college-and-career group at her church. Heidi, my daughter, is a youth and worship leader, and Nicholas, my son, is a worship leader. Jennifer is a schoolteacher. Christy works one-on-one with high schoolers who are disabled. And these are just a few of the many young people who went on missions trips with us as children.

Searching for a Cause to Embrace

In *The Seven Cries of Today's Teens*, Timothy Smith shares about this generation's cry for purpose, adventure, meaning, and intimacy.

> Today's teens are searching for a cause to embrace. They are looking for adventure that demands something from them. So much of their lives have been sanitized from risk and harm that they are looking for ways to "be on the edge" or "push the envelope." This helps explain why millennials have such a high interest in missions. They are willing to give up comfort for a quest with purpose. Some millennials are simply looking for an experience such as snowboarding in the Andes. But when the experience can be supported with an admirable purpose say—snowboarding in the Andes to build relationships with South American teens in order to present Christ to them—then it becomes an adventure.
>
> Without a sense of purpose, teens are left to pursue adventure in less noble ways.
>
> —Timothy Smith, *The Seven Cries of Today's Teens*

Now that you realize the importance of imparting purpose, let's do a little investigating!

FBI Questions:
Uncovering Clues in Your Childhood

1. When you were a child, were you told or did you feel you were made for a special purpose?

2. Did anyone in your life point out special gifts and abilities you had that could bless others?

3. Did you see your parents living with purpose?

4. Did your parents offer you opportunities for noble adventures?

5. What is the first memory you have of reaching out to someone?

6. What special gifts and abilities do you have that could bless others? (Good at finances; great cook; good encourager; great listener; good communicator)

7. If money or time were no object what purposeful thing would you like to do?

FBI Questions:
Uncovering Clues in How You Parent

1. Do your children see you living with specific purpose? (Taking food to a neighbor; taking an elderly person shopping; sponsoring an orphan; feeding the homeless; paying the bills)

2. Do you talk with them about why you are working so hard; why you are paying tithes; why you are sponsoring an orphan; why you are taking food to the neighbor?

3. When you are doing something nice for someone, do you allow your child or loved one to help?

4. What specific gifts and abilities do your children have? (Name each child separately)

5. How could you provide opportunities for your children to use those gifts and abilities to help others?

People who give to others, and live life with purpose, experience fulfillment, a sense of accomplishment, and a sense of value. If you discovered that you don't live as purposefully as you'd like to, don't despair. It's not too late. Ask God to give you eyes and ears to see and hear the needs of others. Begin to listen intently to what people around you are saying and look for ways to bless them. You will be surprised at how many opportunities there are. Don't put it off, just do it. The rewards are life-changing. Now let's look at some simple ideas.

Cracking the Code: Reach Out

There are thousands of ways to provide opportunities for your family to touch the lives of others. Turn the focus off your problems and agendas for the day. Ask God to help you see the pain of others and show you how to carry their burdens. Our actions and attitudes are naturally imparted to our children as they constantly observe our behavior toward others.

Encouraging Your Children

While driving, if I saw an accident, I would pray out loud for the people involved: "Dear God, keep your hand on those involved. I pray for their families. I pray for peace, Amen." My children would agree with my prayer.

One scorching hot day, my children and I were driving to the beach. I noticed a red-faced, sweating, construction worker directing traffic.

"Kids, hand me one of those cold sodas out of the cooler," I said. As we passed by the man, my son handed him a soda, and I smiled, "God bless your day!"

A homeless man once lived in the deserted lot next to our home. When my daughter was about eight, she would see him huddling by a fire.

"Mom, can I take him a little care package?"

"Of course," I replied.

Forty-five minutes later she was heading out the door, arms full of blankets, with two plastic sacks of canned food and a can opener under her arm. She did it all on her own. For the next few years, she was always sneaking things to his little hideaway. Had I discouraged her from reaching out to the homeless man, I could have squelched the deep compassion she had for those in need.

Practical Suggestions

I just don't know what to do or where to start, you might be thinking. First, take advantage of seemingly small, everyday opportunities. Start in little ways: praying with your children for hurting friends; starting a piggy bank for a local homeless shelter. Perhaps you are a little afraid to expose yourself and your family to others' pain, but remember, compassion is birthed in pain!

The following are some more ideas to get your family involved in outreach:

- Sponsor a child in a foreign country (many Christian organizations offer this opportunity)

- Give socks, sleeping bags, and coats to homeless people in your community

- Visit and sing to folks in nursing homes

- Provide transportation to elderly neighbors as they run errands

- Get to know older neighbors: they often need help with simple household chores

- Babysit for needy neighbors

- Deliver food to the housebound

- Visit children's hospitals: get permission beforehand and take pets

- Prepare food boxes for the pantries of community ministries

- Fill individual plastic bags with muffins, juice, granola bars, and fruit; be ready to hand them to homeless people as you drive around your city

- Pray out loud for people while driving; ask your children to pray for stranded motorists, people in an ambulance

- Host an exchange student

- Bake cookies for new neighbors

- Teach English to recent immigrants

- Befriend an international student from a nearby university

- Participate in a missions trip with your family: in your city, across the country, or around the world

Remember Jesus's words: *"It is more blessed to give than to receive"* (Acts 20:35).

On to Clue #5

Way to go! Now that you've uncovered the importance of purpose in our children's lives as well as our own, let's move on to the next clue: the need for support!

From the Heart of an Investigator

When a person lives without purpose, life can seem joyless. I found myself in a dark state after we moved from Oregon to Arizona. I left behind a long-time Bible study group; dear friends; the fun, life-giving church where we had raised our children; my mom and family; close in-laws; and The Bee-Bop Kids ministry. My life went from being warm, rich, and full of love and purpose to being cold, empty, and seemingly pointless.

While raising my children my purpose was to nurture. I so wanted my children to feel loved, experience adventure, and delight in the ways of God. Could I teach them God was real and had a very special plan for their lives? Now that my children were grown and had moved back to Oregon that purpose was gone, and it was painful, frightening.

Our house was deadly quiet. No more roller blades screeching down the hall. I could no longer hear my daughter's finger's gliding over the piano keys or her precious voice dancing through our home as she sang songs of praise and worship. The guitar music coming from my son's room disappeared. No more Portuguese chatter from our Brazilian exchange students; the little neighbor boys stopped ringing the doorbell asking for pickles; the Bee-Bop costumes were packed away; and the phone stopped ringing with calls from my beloved friends. My zest and joy in life gradually disappeared, laughter ceased in our house, and my husband was stuck with a woman he barely recognized, a woman I barely recognized.

I descended into a depression in which I lingered helplessly for a few years. It was only the September 11th attacks, Katie becoming Miss America, and the crisis with my friend's son that jolted me out of that dismal place. I packed my bags and went to my friend's log house in Beavercreek, Oregon, and sought God. Women I loved and who trusted in the Lord were gathered. I entered into a place of worship and prayer. I left the group in the family room, walked into the living room, and stared at the massive stone fireplace.

Standing beneath the skylight, with the sun radiantly beaming down on my head, I looked up to the blue sky and started hashing things out with God: "How did I get to this place, Lord? My life used to be full of life and love and hope. Lord, is my life over? Are You finished with me? Why am I here?"

For over two hours I didn't budge. I stood there with Celtic worship music playing in the background, pleading with God. Slowly, I began to see my life, where I got off track, where I turned the wrong ways, where I was stubborn. It was in this holy, intensely painful place in a quaint log cabin in the woods that I made the pivotal choice to get back in the game and live the life God had intended for me. It started slowly, but gradually God birthed in me a new purpose, a mission to help parents bond deeply with their children, creating a link that will last forever.

I am so thankful for my friend Carol. She captured that moment in a photo of me standing beneath the skylight praying. I look at it everyday and am reminded of the holy moment that changed my life. In the death of the past, God was gracious; a new purpose was birthed.

If God has blessed you with children, then He entrusted them with you for a specific purpose. He hand-picked you for the job. If you're reading this book it's obvious you don't take that job lightly. Be encouraged, embrace the purpose that you were created for: to love God, to love your children and family, and to love the world with purpose. The time you have is fleeting, and take it from me, you can never ever get it back.

 Kid's Clue

"It makes me so happy to see my little brother so happy because of something I gave him."
—Trinity Heinsohn, 5, my granddaughter

CHAPTER 9

Get a Clue #5:

I Need Backup

Uncovering your child's
need for support

---

*"Your love for one another will prove to the world that you
are my disciples."*
—John 13:35 (NLT)

When the planes struck the World Trade Center on
September 11, 2001, we instantly knew our nation
would have to work together to survive. We had to put aside
our differences and support one another. However, in the
beginning, despite the best intentions, hundreds of federal,
state, and city agencies, as well as humanitarian groups,
struggled to learn to work together, and confusion ensued.
But, once the initial problems were worked out, the increased
cooperation and support between groups has only benefited
our country.

If our families are going to survive, we also need to learn to
work together. We need to understand what each family member
needs in the way of support. If we don't know the needs of others,
confusion reigns and it's difficult to create strong bonds.

149

My investigation confirmed that children who didn't feel supported by their parents, or who received inappropriate support, had weaker family bonds. The children I interviewed who didn't feel supported generally gave up; took on a "why bother" attitude—*why should I work so hard at this sport, no one cares*; became depressed and withdrawn—*well, I'm no good anyway*; turned resentful—*they care more about other things than they do me*; and looked for other ways to get attention by behaving badly.

Rene's Story

During one of my FBI Parent Workshops, Rene reflected on a vivid memory of hers from school days.

"We were playing in the volleyball playoffs. Our team worked really hard to get there," Rene said beaming. "As the volleyball was served, I jumped up, blocked the play; it was the game-winning slam. Our team started screaming: 'We won. We won.' The parents were jumping up and down in the bleachers. It was sheer jubilation. One by one, my teammates frantically found their parents. It was very emotional. I searched the seats for my mom or dad."

"They were a no-show again," she continued quietly. "I thought they might surprise me, because I told them it was the championship." She wiped tears from her eyes. "I don't know why I expected them to come; they had never attended one of my games. I stood in the middle of the volleyball court alone. It was awful. One by one, my teammates came up to comfort me. I started crying, not because we won the game but because my parents weren't there to be proud of me, to celebrate with me. It was the most important moment of my life and they didn't care. That's when I realized who my family was, my friends."

"I bet that was awful," I said.

"When I had kids I promised to be at every game," she said smiling. "And I was. I would sit up in the stands screaming frantically at her, 'Way to go, honey; you're the best.' Afterward, she would say, 'Mom, why do you have to embarrass me so much;

I don't want you to come to my games if you can't be quiet.' She stopped telling me when her games were. I had to find out on my own. I figured that I would give her what I had wanted as a child…I guess I went a little overboard."

"I thought the more I screamed and yelled, the more loved she would feel, because that's what I wanted. But now I see how it is pushing her away from me," Rene pondered out loud.

Rene had been a parent for more than ten years and this new revelation was shocking to her. How could she not see something that was so incredibly obvious? She was giving her child something that she had needed as a child, the only problem was her daughter didn't need it or want it, at least not in the same way! Rene's story shows both how important it is for parents to support their children and how important it is for parents to support their children in the best manner for each child.

 FBI Questions:
Uncovering Clues in Your Childhood
Let's see if you can find any valuable revelations from your childhood.

1. What did you *need* from your father (or stepfather) to feel supported when you were a child?

2. Did you *receive* from your father what you needed?

3. What did you *need* from your mother (or stepmother) to feel supported when you were a child?

4. Did you *receive* from your mother what you needed?

5. Who did you feel *the most support* from when you were a child? Why?

6. Who didn't give you support like you *needed* when you were a child?

7. How do you think your experiences as a child affect the way you support your children?

Understanding what you needed to feel supported as a child is important. By understanding your needs as a child, you can begin to distinguish what you needed as a child from what your child needs now. If you understand that, you are better able to connect to your children's hearts.

 FBI Questions:
Uncovering Clues in How You Parent

1. Every child needs something different from each parent. What do your children need from you?

2. How do your children need support from you?

3. What does your child want from you to feel supported? (Name each child individually)

4. How do you show your children you support them?

5. Are you supporting them in the way they need? (Name each child individually)

6. Who would your children say they receive the most support from and why? (Mother, father, stepmother, stepfather, grandparent, aunt, friends, teachers)

7. What changes would you like to make in the way you support your children?

8. Did you discover any new revelations by answering these questions?

Remember, it's your job to use your investigative expertise and discover the individual needs of each of your children.

Special Cases

I have talked to many parents who want to support their children in any way they need, but their occupation makes it virtually impossible. If you are one of those parents, read the following story about John and his mother and learn how she connected with her son even though she couldn't be at every single event.

John was a junior high and high school football player. He was an incredibly well-rounded student. He was also the son of a single mother. While interviewing him he shared: "My mom worked at a bank, I knew she couldn't come to all my games, because if she did, we wouldn't eat. However, on the morning of my game, before she left for work I could see the disappointment in her eyes because she had to miss my game. It was harder on her than it was on me. Just the fact that I knew she really, really wanted to be there made me feel supported."

Rene's parents, mentioned at the beginning of this chapter, never expressed any interest or excitement in what she was doing. They never talked about her wins or defeats, never gave her encouraging phone calls or notes on game day. It was as if what was important to her didn't even exist; the pain of that careless attitude caused her to disconnect from parents. We don't have to go overboard supporting our children. We don't have to be at every game. But what's important to them should be important to us as well. And our kids need to know it.

When you can't be there for your children, tell them how disappointed you are and try one or more of these suggestions:

- Put an encouraging note or special treat in their school bag that morning.

- Make their favorite breakfast the morning of their event.

- Send a loved one to the event in your place and ask them to take photos.

- Celebrate your children's accomplishments or events you missed at a later date with their favorite dessert or dinner.

- Tell them you'll be praying for them during their event, and then ask them how the event went once they return home.

Cracking the Code: Connecting

In terms of support, there are two keys to connecting to the hearts of your children.

1. Listen.
Listen to what your children are telling you they need, both verbally and nonverbally!

Verbal: "Mom, please try to come to the volleyball tournament," "Dad, you can come to my soccer game but please sit with the other parents, and don't scream and yell at the coaches."
Nonverbal: Rolling their eyes, disgusted looks, frowns, sad eyes, tears.

2. Pay attention to their changing needs.
Just when you think you've got them figured out, they'll go and switch on you! As a child, my daughter wanted to be extremely independent. When she was ten, we took a trip to Disney World. She didn't want us around. On every ride, she had to sit in the car in front of us. My son, on the other hand, wanted us close by. He wanted to ride all the rides with us.

When Heidi was a child I supported her by lagging behind her—out of sight—but close enough to help if a problem came up. When Nicholas was a child, I supported him by staying very close and always within sight.

Then, they switched on me, just when I thought I knew how to support each of them. As a teen, Heidi was a singer in the group Knight Voices. She begged me to chaperone every trip.

The following year, Nicholas was in the same group, and he told me he would quit if I chaperoned. I was supporting Heidi by being there. I was supporting Nick by not being there!

That's why it's so important to continue to tune in to your children. They are constantly changing and growing, and if we want to stay connected with them, we must change and grow as well.

Almost There!

Wow, special agent. You've done a lot of incredible investigative work. Hang in there; you're almost done with this case! Pat yourself on the back because you've discovered clue #1, your children's need to trust; clue #2, your children's need to be heard; clue #3, your children's need to be valued and understand their true value; clue #4, your children's need to have purpose not pampering; clue #5, your children's need for specific support. Now, tighten your belt, it's time to move on to our final clue, clue #6, the need for boundaries—not too lenient, not too strict!

From the Heart of An Investigator

When I was a child I wanted my mother to support me by quietly being at my plays, games, or concerts. One Friday night our Milwaukie High Dance Team, of which I was member, was doing the halftime show at a basketball game. As we danced to "Rock Around the Clock," I searched the screaming audience of more than 500 people for my mother's face. She didn't disappoint. Standing in the corner by the door, in her little white Anchorage Restaurant hat and apron, I saw my mother beaming. She had busted her bottom trying to get there in time. It meant so much to me.

On the other hand, my father would often embarrass me if he attended one of my activities. I remember my dad came to a second-grade singing concert wearing a dirty, tight, white T-shirt and two-sizes-too-small black pants that showed his brown socks crinkled around his ankles. If that weren't bad enough, he was drunk. I learned at a young age never to tell him about any of my upcoming events, and I swore my mother to secrecy. While my father is somewhat of an extreme example, it is important that parents provide support in an appropriate way, one that is sensitive to the child's perspective.

Our children need our support, our concern, and our interest. We also need to be sensitive and respectful enough of our children to learn how to provide support in the specific ways that each child needs. My prayer for you is that through this chapter you have discovered powerful insight into what your children need from you to feel supported!

 Kid's Clue

"I was so scared to get on the inner tube and have the boat pull me, but I did. And guess what? I scared my fear away!"
—Joshua Goddard, 6, my grandson

CHAPTER 10

Get a Clue #6:

Mama, Don't...
I Mean Do...Fence Me In

Uncovering your child's need
for specific boundaries—
not too lenient, not too strict

---

*The boundary lines have fallen for me in pleasant places;
surely I have a delightful inheritance!*
—Psalm 16:6 (NIV)

We need to keep things that will nurture us inside our fences and keep things that will harm us outside. In short, boundaries help us keep the good in and the bad out.
—Henry Cloud and John Townsend, *Boundaries*

Investigators have to know the law. When they are working their cases, they have to know what they can do and what they can't do. For all citizens, laws, rules, and boundaries are put into place to help us understand what jurisdiction and access we have in other's lives and what jurisdiction and access we allow others to have in ours. If the boundaries are crystal-clear, we can be assured of peace, safety, and security; if they're not clear, fear, confusion, and instability reign.

157

Who's the Boss?

My day flipped from tranquil to traumatic with five little words, "Trinity, time for your nap." While their mother, my daughter-in-law, went to get a massage, I watched my grandchildren, Trinity, two, and Isaiah, seven months, on a sunny, 95-degree Arizona morning. We pranced around as princess and queen, colored red and green, and played other games. After several fun-filled hours, Trinity rubbed her eyes and yawned. Isaiah started to cry. Naptime was drawing near.

"Trinity, it's time for your nap," I said walking toward the bathroom. She looked startled. "Let's go potty."

"No, Gamma; no bedtime," she said defiantly with furrowed brows. She didn't budge. I didn't budge. We were like two Wild West cowboys facing each other just before the gun fight.

"Trinity, it's nap time," I insisted. With her hands on her hips she took one step forward, like she was going to draw her pistol. I waited. She took one step, then another, and stomped right by me. As I helped her onto the toilet, she scowled. She sat down, flung her two-year-old head forward, and flipped her moppy brown hair toward the floor.

"Gamma, I no go to bed," she said peeking through her hair.

"Trinity, yes, you are going to go to bed," I smiled.

Abruptly she jerked her head back, whipping my legs with her hair like a horse swatting flies with his tail. She pushed her nose in the air and rolled her bottom lip under like a little, fat Tootsie Roll. She then arched her back gripping the toilet with both hands like she was preparing for a possible launch, and let out a bloodcurdling scream, "I want my mommy."

I was stunned. I was shocked. How could that enormous sound come out of this sweet little child? Before I knew what hit me, she flipped a switch and began launching tsunami-size tears. They popped out of her eyes like popcorn, gaining fierce speed racing toward the tile floor where they silently exploded.

As I carried her to her bed I could hear Isaiah crying in the living room. I gently tried to lay her down, but she wasn't going down easily. She buried her face in the pillows but quickly and defiantly shot her little bottom into the air, knees curled under.

I knew what she was thinking, *I'm lying down on the outside but standing up on the inside.*

My neck grew hot. I thought, *I'm not cut out for this.*

"I no go to bed, Gamma. I want my mommy!"

"Trinity," I said sternly in a low voice. "You are going to go to sleep." It was obvious she wasn't used to me telling her no.

"Waaa. I want my mommy. I want my mommy," she insistently cried.

"Trinity, Grandma is going to go put brother to bed, and when you stop crying I'll come back and read you a story." She ignored me, raising her bottom higher.

"I want my mommy. I want my mommy," she said over and over not missing a breath. As I quickly tried to escape the room I tripped over her doll. Seeing Isaiah screaming on the floor, I picked him up and tried to calm him down. For the next 15 minutes I was serenaded by a rousing rendition of "Dueling Banjos" without banjos—just screams. Isaiah finally fell asleep while Trinity kept her not-so-precious serenade going.

"I want my mommy; I want my mommy," she cried in a state of delirium. Where she got all the energy to keep her party going, I'll never know.

"If you quiet down I will read you a story." She kept sobbing. I walked out of the room, praying she'd cry herself to sleep. Her cries got stronger. Fifteen minutes later I tromped back in the battle. Her little bottom was still pointing toward the ceiling, and she was desperately grasping her tear-stained pillow.

"I want my mommy." I lay down with her. "I want my mommy." I started lightly scratching her back. "I want my mommy." Slowly she closed her eyes. "I want my mo—mm—y." Her words got softer and slower. I started counting, "I want my mommy, 146, I want my mommy, 147, I want my mommy, 148." Soon I lost count. She was lulling me to sleep. Slurring her words together she began mumbling like she was drunk. "I wan mam; I wan mam; I wan mammam." It sounded so funny that

I giggled. This startled her and her "mama momentum" revved up again. Gently scratching her back I quietly sang, "Hush, little baby, don't you cry." We became quite the duet. After 45 agonizing minutes, she lay peacefully asleep.

I won! I carefully rolled off the bed, slithered to her door, and crawled to the kitchen praying neither child would wake up. I felt shell-shocked. I got up on my feet, stumbled to the counter, and that's when I spotted them—a full jar of M&M's. I was shaking as I opened the jar and began popping the candies in my mouth. As I flopped on the couch, I thought about the millions of men and women around the world who do this every day. Parents who know it would be easier to give up but who stay the course. I lifted my jar into the air, "Here's to all the parents in the world!" and tossed back ten more scrumptious M&M's.

What If She'd Won?
At two years old, Trinity was learning about boundaries. Hers and mine.

What would have happened if I had given in and let Trinity win? It would've been easier on me, but I'd have led her to believe she was in control, that her behavior could manipulate me (and other adults). Now, a one-time lack of discipline on my part may not have scarred Trinity for life, but if her parents were to frequently give into her whining it could have serious consequences.

Trinity's act was the 2-year-old version of a temper tantrum. What does the 10-year-old version look like? Possibly a child bullying anyone who disagrees with what she wants to do. What does the 18-year-old version sound like? "I'm taking your car because you can't tell me what to do." What does the 28-year-old version sound like? "I'm not going to work today because I don't feel like it." What does the 44-year-old version sound like? "Nobody tells me what to do," he says after being fired for the umpteenth time. If our children aren't taught about boundaries and rules at a young age, it is quite possible they will grow up confused emotionally, physically, and spiritually.

Why Do We Need Boundaries?

Since the beginning of time God has given us boundaries. Eat anything you like, except the fruit from the tree of the knowledge of good and evil. Have no other gods, do not murder, do not steal—the Ten Commandments. Then there are many beautiful proverbs. Finally, we have Jesus summarizing the law, telling us to love God and love our neighbors. All of these wise rules, boundaries, and laws are intended to help us live the kind of beautiful life that comes from surrendering to God and desiring to glorify Him. In Deuteronomy 28 all of the blessings that come with obedience to God's commands are revealed.

> *"Now it shall come to pass, if you diligently obey the voice of the LORD your God, to observe carefully all His commandments which I command you today, that the LORD your God will set you high above all nations of the earth. And all these blessings shall come upon you and overtake you, because you obey the voice of the LORD your God."*
> —Deuteronomy 28:1–2

The Scriptures then go on to say how we will be blessed in the city and the country, in the fruit of our body, the produce of our ground, the increase of our cattle, the offspring of our flocks, our baskets, and our kneading bowl. We will be blessed when we come in and when we go out. The Lord will cause our enemies to be defeated, and our storehouses will be blessed. He will open up His heavens, give rain for our land, and bless the work of our hands. (See Deuteronomy 28:1–14.)

I don't know about you, but I would love to live with these incredible treasures. God gives us boundaries to protect us, and when we honor them, we submit to His authority. And this is the path of life and of blessing.

Here are three common statements I heard from adult children concerning boundaries. Do you identify with any of these?

- "My parents were too strict. They never gave me any choices and rarely let me do anything with other kids. I guess they didn't trust me. I felt like I was in prison."

- "My parents were too lenient. I pretty much did what I wanted. It didn't seem like anyone really cared about me." "My mom was into her own thing. She let me do anything I wanted as long as I didn't bother her."

- "My mother gave me boundaries that my father didn't enforce. She was strict; he was lenient. I learned to manipulate and get what I wanted early."

Now let's go deeper.

1. When you were a child, did your parents place boundaries on what you were allowed to say or talk about?

Mother: *"We don't talk about others like that."* Or, *"Honey, you know we don't talk about Daddy's alcoholism."*

Father: *"Son, it's OK to swear, just not around women."*

2. Did your parents have boundaries on what they said or talked about?

3. When you were a child did your parents place boundaries on how you were allowed to express feelings?

Mother: *"Stop crying or I'll give you something to cry about."* Or, *"I understand that you're upset. Can you settle down and tell me why you are crying?*

Father: *"Don't be such a baby; boys don't cry."* Or, *"I'm sorry your sister took your toy, but you shouldn't hit her."*

4. Did your parents have boundaries on how they expressed feelings?

5. When you were a child, were there boundaries put on what you ate?
Mother: *"Stop eating those chips!"* Or, *"Clean your plate or no dessert!"*
Father: *"Son, have another steak; real men eat beef."*

6. When you were a child did your parents put boundaries on what they ate?

7. When you were a child were you allowed to look at whatever you wanted?
Mother: *"Please don't watch that television show!"*
Father: *"You shouldn't be looking at that magazine, those images will stay in your mind forever!"*

8. Did your parents have boundaries in what they watched or read?

9. Overall, did your parents consistently reinforce the rules they set in your home?

10. Did you get conflicting messages from your parents concerning what was accepted and what wasn't?

11. If your parents modeled inconsistent boundaries, how did that make you feel?

Hopefully, these questions were enlightening. Perhaps you discovered that you are still reacting to the harsh boundaries your parents placed around you. Perhaps you discovered that your parents' boundaries were too lenient, allowing you too much freedom. Perhaps you discovered that your parents didn't live with the same healthy boundaries they expected from you.

Maybe they even encouraged you to have unhealthy boundaries. Whatever you discovered, my prayer is that you process this information, recognizing it as part of your life story and a unique opportunity for growth.

If you reflect and see that the boundaries modeled and taught to you were consistent and fair, you are blessed. Our goal as parents should be to consistently and fairly set boundaries that, borrowing from the three bears, are "just right."

FBI Questions: Uncovering Clues in How You Parent

Now let's look at what boundaries look, sound, taste, and feel like to you and your children!

1. As an adult, do you have clear boundaries for how you talk to the following people? *(respectfully or sarcastically, gently or harshly, loudly or softly, rudely or kindly)*
    Spouse: Children:
    (Ex-spouse):   Co-workers/friends:
    Parents:

2. Do you have clear boundaries for how you allow the following people to talk to you? *(respectfully or sarcastically, gently or harshly, loudly or softly, rudely or kindly)*
    Spouse: Children:
    (Ex-spouse):   Co-workers/friends:
    Parents:

3. Do you have boundaries for how you allow your children to talk to you and others? What are they? Do your children know what those boundaries are?

4. As an adult, do you have boundaries for what you allow yourself to look at?

5. Do you have boundaries for what you allow your children to look at?

6. Do your children know what those boundaries are?

7. As an adult, are you pleased with the boundaries you have for yourself for what you put in your mouth? *(food, alcohol, beverages, cigarette)*

8. Do you have boundaries for what you allow your children to consume?

9. Do your children know what those boundaries are?

10. As an adult, do you have boundaries for yourself on what you listen to? *(CDs, radio stations, television, gossip)*

11. Do you have boundaries for what you allow your children to listen to?

12. Do your children know what those boundaries are?

13. What are your behaviors teaching your children about boundaries?

Remember these questions aren't posed to make you feel badly about yourself; they are intended to help you see how you look through the eyes of your children. Take what you learned and let it motivate you to change the things you need to change. Trust God. He is there every step to guide you and me!

Riding Lessons

OK, so what next? Perhaps we can find the answer in the horse-and-rider relationship. Cowgirls and cowboys are definitely their own breed. They talk their own language, wear fancy cowboy boots and hats, and have their own style of clothes. They walk with a certain strut, drive big 'ol 4x4 pickup trucks, but more important, many have learned a secret that the rest of us desperately need to understand.

"Help me; somebody help me," Marie shrieked in horror.

"Pull on the reins. Make him stop!" Jenni yelped.

"He won't stop. He won't stop," Marie yelled desperately. The faster the horse ran, the harder she pulled on the reins. The horse came to an abrupt skidding halt, nearly throwing her to the ground. Marie continued to pull back on the reins. The horse's muscular legs began stepping backwards, gaining speed with every step, stopping as he thrust his front legs wildly into the air like the Black Stallion.

"Help me; please, help me," Maria shrieked trying desperately to stay on the horse.

"Let go of the reins, let go of the reins," Jenni screamed breathlessly as she approached the horse. "He thinks you're telling him to go backwards."

Marie dropped the reins from her clutching hands, and the horse came to an abrupt halt. She sat trembling on the horse.

"Now slowly pick up the reins," Jenni calmly stated.

Carefully Marie bent over to grab the reins and the horse took off again.

"Marie, tighten the reins, but don't pull too hard, because then you are signaling him to back up." Marie gently pulled the reins toward her chest. "Now don't give him any slack."

Slowly she pulled on the reins, and immediately the horse stopped, and didn't budge. Marie sat apprehensively on the horse for several minutes.

"OK, now that he realizes you're in control, slowly let out the reins," Jenni gently encouraged.

Hesitantly, Marie let out the reins and began trotting about. She repeated this process—pulling the reins in and letting them out—over and over for the next several minutes. Jenni excitedly jumped on her horse and trotted up to Marie, "That's what I call happy time, when the horse does what we want."

She went on, "The horse is happy and you're happy. But when he disobeys, it's unhappy time, and we tighten the ropes until he obeys, until he learns who's in control."

At first, Marie didn't trust her horse; her horse didn't trust her. Both horse and rider were receiving mixed messages; both were afraid. Confusion, fear, and frustration ruined what potentially could have been an incredible ride. When they both knew who was in charge, everything changed...for the better.

In the same way, we need to establish a high level of trust with our children by establishing our parental authority in a godly way and setting fair boundaries. We need to parent consistently, tightening and relaxing the "reins" in a manner suited to and understood by each of our children. When our children get mixed messages from us—by being strict one day because we're in a bad mood, and lenient another because we're in a good mood—it causes them incredible frustration and confusion. It breeds mistrust. The boundary lines are always shifting, and they don't know what's expected from them.

When I was a child, I knew exactly what the boundaries were when my mother was home: be at the dinner table at six fifteen, go to bed by nine, and be up at seven. Those boundaries rarely wavered. When my father was home and watching me, the boundaries flew out the window. He let us pretty much have free reign as long as it didn't interfere with what he wanted to do. One year he quit drinking for about 11 months. All of a sudden he ruled with an iron fist. He was strict, unreasonable, and no fun. He had trained us for 17 years to have a lot of a freedom, and now that we were teenagers, he suddenly wanted to tighten the reins. We were all miserable.

Children need to know that we are in control, that we know what we are doing. However, there is a fine line between holding the reins too tightly and holding the reins too loosely. Too tight, they rebel. Too loose, they feel unsafe and insecure. Cowboys and girls have to know their horses; we have to know our children. Each horse is different; each child is different.

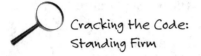

Cracking the Code:
Standing Firm

So, let's consider the practical application of these principles. How do you know if you're being too strict or too lenient? How do you find the fine line?

I looked to horse riding again. This time the answer came in the form of a 4-foot-8-inch, 80-pound, blue-eyed, blonde-haired, cowboy-hat-wearing, big-shiny-silver-belt-buckled, 12-year-old cowgirl. I was struck how tiny she was as she sat atop her 2,000-pound, black-and-white Arabian stallion. I couldn't keep my eyes off her. I watched in awe as her tiny body guided her horse to side-step poles, gracefully race around barrels, and masterfully jump logs. I was stumped, as I couldn't see how she was giving her horse commands.

"She looks like she's eight years old on that massive horse. How can she have such beautiful control of that huge animal?" I whispered to my friend Susie as we shivered in the icy barn, waiting for her daughter, Molly, to compete in the Mt. Hood Equestrian Show.

"It's amazing isn't it?" she said, pulling her thick wool blanket tight. "She's giving him commands, a click, click with her tongue or a flinch of her thighs."

I could see my breath as I squinted trying to see the tiniest movement. "When I was a 25-year-old mother of two 30-pound toddlers I couldn't get my children to pick up their toys. What in the world has she learned at 12 that I still haven't?"

"These little girls love their horses," Susie said trying to get warm by scooting closer to the propane heater. "They grow up with them. Some have been out in the barns tinkering with horses since they could walk. By being extremely disciplined, feeding and watering their horses, mucking stalls, grooming, shampooing, combing, brushing and braiding their tails, they've formed deep bonds with their horses.

"If the rider is going to raise an extremely obedient horse, she can't allow other things to take up her time like running to the mall without feeding them or talking on the phone for hours with friends."

"Wow, sounds like an awful lot of work to me, but what an incredibly beautiful thing," I said still watching in awe.

"These little girls really know their horses. They know what spooks them. They know when they are nervous. They know what makes their horses happy. They know their horses, because they spend hours and hours with them, cleaning, grooming, and training them."

"That is such a big responsibility," I said.

"Have you ever seen Molly train Harley? She holds a rope tight to his harness and gradually lets the rope out as he does what she wants him to do. When she sees her horse automatically respond to her commands, she lets the rope out further. She does the same maneuver over and over until he gets it. They have developed a strong bond of trust, because she trains him through encouraging pats on his side, scratching his neck and ears, consistent boundaries. I've never heard her rant and rave at him, she talks to him lovingly, 'Good boy,' and 'That's right; good job.' He's getting consistent commands so he's not confused. She doesn't move on to the next stage until he masters the last," Susie said proudly. "As she does this an amazing thing happens: Harley wants to please Molly."

"I've seen how focused and disciplined Molly has become as she's learning how to train him. I'm so proud of her," I said.

"I've seen girls who are mean to their horses and beat and neglect them. Those horses become mean and distrustful. I've also seen girls who let their horses run wild—and the horses are just that—wild and unridable. The girls who win the blue ribbons have learned some vitally important secrets: knowing their horse, grooming them with love, guiding them patiently and consistently, giving them consistent commands, and giving them equal amounts of encouragement and praise."

Still Confused?

OK, so what if your child is bucking you every time you put limits on her? Perhaps her behavior screams, "I hate you, I want nothing to do with you." Be encouraged, you can get through it. Drs. Henry Cloud and John Townsend in the book *Boundaries with Kids* give us some wise advice.

> The parent who cannot tolerate being hated will not be able to provide the reality the child needs to overcome feeling entitled. Love and limits are the most important qualities for a parent. The ability to tolerate being hated and seen as "bad" is a parent's next most important quality. God, as the ultimate parent, is able to do what is right and to take a stand, no matter what anyone thinks of him. He loves, but he has his standards and keeps them, even when we do not like it. If he did not, the universe would be in trouble. One of the great lessons of the book of Job is that no matter what Job thought of God, God did not strike back at him or cease to be God. The same is true for a parent. You need to be able to contain the protest, stay connected, not strike back, and remain the parent.
>
> —Henry Cloud and John Townsend, *Boundaries with Kids*

I don't like to be hated. I hate being hated. But for the benefit of my children I have, at times, endured it. Cloud and Townsend add, "Children think that their anger is more powerful than it really is, that it has the power to destroy you. They need to learn that you are bigger than their feelings so they can learn to be bigger than their feelings as well." As the two authors suggest, we must empathize with our children's anger and frustration at limits without getting angry ourselves. We can remain both loving and firm. Our self-control keeps the situation from getting out of hand.

When my children were bucking boundaries, at times I felt I had failed miserably. I reacted in many unhelpful ways: I got angry, attacked them, gave them the silent treatment, acted devastated by their actions, and compared them to good children. (Cloud and Townsend identify these as negative responses in their book). And no surprise, my kids disconnected from me at those times. However my husband stayed loving but firm. He was secure in his decisions. They got mad at me, but not at him.

Dr. Foster Cline and Jim Fay share this nugget:

> When a crisis erupts, we should take a moment, pray, breathe deeply, relax, write down all possible options, talk them over with a person we respect, think about our ability to cope with the worst possible outcome and keep the faith. After all, that's our best weapon.
> —Foster Cline and Jim Fay, *Parenting with Love and Logic*

Keep the faith; it's our best weapon. Only God can help us set the loving boundaries our children need.

Congratulations!

You've done it! You've just uncovered the six clever clues to your children's hearts. You've searched for truth, followed the leads, found the missing links, and learned to be trustworthy; you've discovered the importance of listening to what your child is trying to tell you; you've found the treasures in true value; you've accepted the mission to help your children live a purposeful life; you've learned how to support your child; and you've discovered the importance of creating child-specific boundaries. So, now is the mission accomplished, the case closed?

From the Heart of an Investigator

When our children are grown, and especially when they begin families of their own, the tables turn, and they will need to set boundaries with us. It can be just as painful to us when they set limits as it was for them to have limits as children.

As I shared earlier in the book, I was confused and devastated when my daughter walked away from me emotionally and physically for a time. However, I have come to a deeper understanding as to why it happened: she was setting her own boundaries.

As her own family grew, she needed to limit the outside influences in her life, and that included my husband and me. She turned her phone off for most of the day, limited the time she spent with friends, and increased the time she spent focusing on her kids and husband. Everything she gave a little time to took something away from her family, and she realized she wasn't willing to make that sacrifice. By exercising her right to say no to people and opportunities, and by picking and choosing events she wants her family involved in, she is saying yes to her children. She is getting to know every flinch of her "little horses." As she gets to know them better, she is better able to set child-specific boundaries.

My hope is that this chapter has helped you realize how your daily choices either enhance your life or take something from it. Unfortunately, for the many grown children I interviewed, the little choices their parents made every day made life difficult for them. Like my face-off with Trinity at the beginning of the chapter, remember when your child screams, "I no go to bed," take the time and do the work of lovingly sticking to fair boundaries. You will be amazed at the beautiful rewards you reap, not to mention the yummy M&M's.

 Kid's Clue

"If Mom says no, go ask your dad while he's listening to baseball."
—Laura Grina, 10, (me)

CHAPTER 11

Case Closed:

Mission Accomplished,
or Is It?

To everything there is a season, a time for every purpose under heaven.
—Ecclesiastes 3:1

Throughout this book you and I have both been challenged to investigate our lives and the lives of our children. As we've dug, poked, and prodded, we have discovered hidden mysteries and treasures. Some revelations were delightfully precious gems. Others seemed a little more like fool's gold as our investigation revealed how we've bought into some counterfeit beliefs and behaviors. No matter what you discovered, it has brought insight into your heart as well as your child's.

Jesus tells us that the kingdom of heaven is like treasure hidden in a field. (See Matthew 13:44.) The fact that it is hidden suggests that to find it we must hunt for it and seek it out. If we want strong relationships with our children throughout their lives, we must use our investigative resources and continue to hunt for hidden treasures. And even then, as we stated in the first chapter, we can be the best parents in the world, do the investigative work, and still raise children who walk away. Ultimately, our children have the freedom to choose the road they want to travel.

One of The Bee-Bop Kids' more unusual sketches featured four sets of identical twins. Yes, don't choke; it's no joke. I had the privilege of directing four sets of identical twins—Kevin and Kyle, 7; Jack and Jason, 9; Brianna and Becky, 16; and the oldest, Dave and Steve, 18. The sketch begins with one of each of the four sets of twins standing on the stage wearing white. The audience can't see the hidden identical twin behind them wearing black. When Amy Grant's song "Shadows" begins to play—"*There are two of me, one does the right thing, one cannot see*"—the twin behind, wearing black, pokes his head out. Throughout the rest of the sketch, the sets of children portray the war between good and evil that goes on inside of us all. It was a very powerful visual.

When these sets of twins graduated from high school, in some instances, one of the them continued to embrace their parents' convictions while the other did not. The magic question: Why? And that is the question we have been trying to answer throughout this entire book.

Our children have the freedom to choose what road they want to take: some choose the route of the world and some choose the route to God. Something clicked in each of the twins that either sold them on what their parents were trying to instill in them or turned them away. The good news is, at any time, our children, like ourselves, can change directions—they can choose to switch roads. That is why it's important to keep praying, for your heart as well as your child's. Just because their behavior is screaming one thing doesn't mean it will always stay that way. We have hope! There are seasons in all of our lives, and seasons change.

Seasons of Parenting

I, like you, have gone through and will continue to go through seasons with my children. The good news and the bad news is…seasons change. God made us to grow throughout life, and traveling through seasons with our children is a part of it. The hope we have in thriving and surviving through the seasons lies in the word *traveling*. Don't stop. Continue on. Keep moving. The 23rd Psalm says, "*Yea, though I walk through the valley of the shadow of death, I will fear no evil*" (v. 4). The key is to "walk through"… continue on, don't get stuck.

• *Hoorah for Summer*
When my children were little—I called it the summer season—most days were sunny and warm. They clung to me like koala cubs to their mother. I saw the sun shining in their eyes; I could do no wrong. Life was cozy and playful. Most days we'd wrap our arms around one another and rub noses. They delighted in me and I in them. One day while we were basking in the sun's warmth, I could feel a chill ripple through the air. The tree began to sway as a cold breeze blew. The days became a little shorter. My snuggly koala cubs were growing and were not so comfortable in my arms anymore.

• *The Chill of Fall*
Then came autumn. The leaves began to shake, the winds to howl. Some days my cubs buried their heads in my chest and snuggled. Other days their claws came out and they didn't want anything to do with me. They pushed away, trying to escape the confinement of my safe, loving arms. Carelessly, they crawled down from the tree. They wandered away, taking their gentle spirits with them. The more they grew and explored the world around them, the less they wanted from me.

• *The Bite of Winter*
Soon it's cold, dark, and windy. I don't know where my precious cubs have gone. It's lonely and the days have become so long. My heart is breaking. I am confused. I frantically search everywhere. The long days of numbing cold slowly sap the life out of me. It seems winter will go on forever. I'm exhausted.

I give up searching for them and quietly search myself. *What have I done wrong? What will I change if they ever come back?* I face the good, the bad, and the difficult. I hang my head in grief. No strength to look up. As I knew it, my relationship with my children dies.

But wait, what is that I glimpse on the horizon? I sit up straight, squinting to see if this is my imagination. Could it be? Is it possible? I stand still for a second trying to focus, and slowly walk toward the movement. Squinting, I feel a ray of sun peek through the dark clouds and caress my shoulder, encouraging me to continue in the deep frigid snow. The snow melts the further I walk. Yes, it is our man-cub. But wait, he's so big—is it him?

- *Spring Arrives!*

As we embrace, we're different. I gaze longingly into my little koala's eyes, and yes, there it is, the long lost twinkle I so desperately missed. He's grown; he's changed. My she-cub arrives. We embrace. She's grown; she's changed. They notice that I've changed. *Is it safe to climb the tree together again?* My koala cubs break the embrace, slowly walk away, and begin climbing their own trees. I turn slowly and walk to mine.

As I climb my tree, I lovingly look over my shoulder and flash my cubs a comforting grin. I sit nestled on my branch and I thank God that winter is over; spring is here. My cubs have come back—not to my home—but in my heart.

New Life in Death

I have gone through all four seasons with my children (more than once), and I have survived. You can too! I found a valuable key in the midst of one winter season. When my daughter walked away from her father and me for a time, we were dumbfounded.

It hurt. We cried. We got angry. We clung to Proverbs 3:5-6, *"Trust in the LORD with all your heart, and lean not on your own understanding. In all your ways acknowledge Him, and He shall direct your paths."* We had no choice but to trust God with all our hearts, because we truly didn't understand what was happening. We struggled to acknowledge Him in all of our ways, and when we did, He directed our path. He comforted us, He loved us, and He corrected us. Through this remarkable process, we surrendered.

In the Old Testament, God asked Abraham to surrender his only son and place him on an altar. *"Take now your son, your only son Isaac, whom you love, and go to the land of Moriah, and offer him there as a burnt offering on one of the mountains of which I shall tell you"* (Genesis 22:2). Abraham did as he was told, and when he was about to sacrifice his son, the Lord provided a ram for the offering.

> *"Then the angel of the LORD called to Abraham a second time out of heaven, and said: 'By Myself I have sworn, says the LORD, because you have done this thing, and have not withheld your son, your only son—blessing I will bless you, and multiplying I will multiply your descendants as the stars of the heaven and as the sand which is on the seashore; and your descendants shall possess the gate of their enemies. In your seed all the nations of the earth shall be blessed because you have obeyed My voice.'"*
> —Genesis 22:15–18

Abraham experienced tremendous blessing as he laid Isaac on God's altar. God never intended our children to be ours to keep forever. He loans them to us for a very short part of their lives.

Tiffany's Story of Surrender

"Push, push," her birthing coach had said excitedly. "I see the top of his head; look at all that black hair! One more big push and he'll be out!"

And with one more great big breath, Tiffany gave birth to eight-pound-three-ounce baby boy Tyler. She gently cradled him in her arms and kissed his wrinkled face.

"You're beautiful," she whispered into his ear. She caressed his tiny head; a love she had never known flooded her soul. Tears streamed from her eyes as she touched his soft skin and counted his tiny fingers and toes.

The Countdown Begins
- *Twenty-four hours from now my life will drastically change,* she thought. *Do I have the courage to go through with this?*

She meticulously examined his tiny fingers, tracing them over and over, memorizing every wrinkle. He had such big hands for such a little man.

- *Twenty hours to go.*

As she laid him next to her, she couldn't quit staring at him, touching him.

There was a knock at the door. "Can I come in?" the adoptive mother asked nervously.

"Sure, come on in. He's sleeping," Tiffany responded. "Do you want to hold him?"

- *Fifteen hours to go.*

"Look at all that dark hair," his adoptive father said nervously as he gently laid him back in Tiffany's arms.

- *Twelve hours to go.*

"Mom, you have to stop crying, please," Tiffany said, frustrated.

"I don't want you to do this," her mother cried. On the verge of becoming hysterical, she said, "You don't have to do this; I'll adopt him."

"I can't handle you right now, Mom; please can you go in the waiting room?" Tiffany said boldly, thinking to herself: *This isn't what I need right now...I have to do this; this is his best chance.*

- *Ten hours to go.*

Tiffany drifted off to sleep to the rhythm of her newborn's breathing.

- *Six hours to go.*
  "Do you need anything?" the nurse asked sweetly.
  "I would love something to eat," Tiffany quietly answered, never taking her eyes off her baby.

- *Three hours to go.*
  "Can you hold him? I need to go get cleaned up," she said as she handed him over to Sarah, her birthing coach. *Tick, tock, tick, tock...* the clock subtly antagonized as she solemnly walked to the bathroom.

- *Two hours to go.*
  She turned on the faucet and quietly waited for the tub to fill. As her toe hit the steaming hot water, one lonely tear rolled down her nose and splashed into the bath. She slid into the water and began to ponder the moment of surrender waiting on the other side of the door. As her body relaxed, her prayers came as fast and furious as the shower of tears invading the tub.

  "Heavenly Father," she cried, "I give You my precious baby boy." She covered her face trying to quiet her sobs. "I pray for his new mommy and daddy and his two sisters. I pray that they will have overwhelming love for him like I do." She didn't bother to wipe the snot from her nose. "I trust that they will give him all the things I can't."

  Sobs wrenched her body. She tried to catch her breath; time was running out. "I pray for his first day of kindergarten, that You will protect him and keep him safe. I pray for his first birthday party, I pray for his first day of soccer practice. I trust You Lord to hold him when he is discouraged, to embrace him when he is afraid."

  The blinding tears stung her eyes. "I trust You to hold him all the Christmases that I can't. Please protect him when he is learning to ride his first bike."

  Desperately she tried to catch her breath, "I trust You to be with him on graduation, because I can't be. I trust You to direct him when he goes off to college." The longer she prayed, the weaker she felt. "I trust You to give him wisdom when he has his first girlfriend. And when he gets married, Lord, please bring him the wife You created for him."

"Lord, be with his children and grandchildren. Let them know Your love. I trust You to speak to him in the quietness of his heart, to be real to him, to be more than just a Sunday School story." Drained and exhausted, Tiffany continued to mumble out prayers, desperately asking the Lord to care for the baby she loved. As she did this, she slowly drifted to sleep with a broken heart in a tub of broken dreams.

- *One hour to go.*
  Sarah knocked on the door. "Are you OK?"
  "Yeah, I'll be out in a minute." Tiffany shivered as she awoke in the tepid bath. She felt God's overwhelming presence, "Now you know how much I love you."

She closed her eyes as she recited the verse seared in her heart. John 3:16: *"For God so loved the world that He gave His only begotten Son, that whoever believes in Him should not perish but have everlasting life."* She thought, *You gave Your one and only Son that I would have life, and have it abundantly.* This powerful Scripture, which she had known most of her life, suddenly took on new meaning.

"God, You are real. God, I know You are going to take care of baby Tyler. God I know You will take care of me," Tiffany said to Him with a new sense of confidence. "God, thank You for touching my life; thank You for touching my son and keeping him in the palm of Your hand."

As she rose out of her bath, she left confusion and debilitating fear floating in the tub. She felt enveloped in peace, a peace that for 20 years had eluded her. A burden had been lifted. Her heart had been washed clean, and the truth became clear. She would always be united with her son, forever in her heart, and connected through her prayers, even if she never saw him or touched him again. She wrapped the towel around her body—a warmth and peace wrapped around her and flooded her soul. She felt enveloped in God's love and peace.

- *Fifteen minutes left.*

Tiffany got dressed and packed her things. Baby Tyler's new mom and dad entered the room with the birthing coach for one last moment together. As they all sat admiring this bundle of joy, tightly wrapped in a soft blue blanket, everyone knew it was time.

"Thank you for trusting us with this little boy," the adoptive mom said as she choked back tears.

"I know he will be in good hands," Tiffany responded with a quivering voice.

As she held tiny Tyler in her arms one last time, she gave him one last kiss on the forehead and sweetly whispered, "Goodbye, Tyler. I love you. You're in good hands. God bless you little man."

A nurse appeared in the doorway with a wheelchair. The time had come. Tiffany gently lay him down in the bassinet and turned to the adoptive parents. She gave them a lingering hug.

"Thank you," she whispered. As she was wheeled through the double doors, she knew it was finished. She had done it. She had given him life. The life he deserved.

Tiffany experienced an overwhelming peace, because she surrendered. She surrendered her child, for his good, for his benefit. And as she surrendered his life, as well as her own, God gave her something she wasn't expecting, a wealth of assurance and peace that He will take care of both Tyler and her.

Tiffany gets yearly updates and pictures of Tyler and his family. He is growing up to be a handsome little man. Tiffany serves in her church and longs to disciple young women in similar situations. She is now happily married to a strong Christian man, and they are raising my two gorgeous grandchildren. Yes, she married my son!

Time Is Tickin'!

God is calling us to trust Him as we travel through seasons with our children. His call is the same no matter how long we have them: one short day like Tiffany, or 18 quickly fleeting years.

As we surrender our children, we truly learn what trusting God looks and feels like. Surrender is a process. It needs to be done continually—monthly, weekly, daily, hourly, and sometimes minute to minute. When we trust God with our children, we experience a peace and assurance that can only come through Him. He carried Tiffany when she let go of her baby boy. He has been there every step of her walk, and He will be there every step of yours. He will guide you through the parenting maze, and as He does, He will abundantly bless you with wisdom, knowledge, and insight, especially when you feel anything but wise, knowledgeable, or insightful. When we give up our children, He gives us full assurance that our children are His children and He will take care of them. Will you let Him?

From the Heart of an Investigator

As your investigative journey comes to an end, I want to congratulate you. You have courageously and bravely searched for truth, the whole truth, and nothing but the truth in your childhood and in how you are raising your children, and you've survived. You've followed the leads, found the missing links, and made incredible changes: forgiving your parents and yourself for not being perfect. You have discovered what life looks like through the eyes of your children, and now you're better able to understand how to connect to their hearts.

I pray that as you travel through the many changing seasons of your children's lives, no matter their age, you will continue to remember and practice the six clever clues:

Clue #1: You will meet their need to trust by living a trustworthy life.

Clue #2: You will meet their need to be heard, by zipping your mouth and being a great listener.

Clue #3: You will meet their need to be valued by understanding what makes them feel valuable and teaching them they are valuable because they are God's child.

Clue #4: You will meet their need to have purpose, by living a purposeful life and helping them see and understand their purpose.

Clue #5: You will meet their need to be supported by understanding what they need from you in the way of support.

Clue #6: You will meet their need to have specific, fair, and consistent boundaries at every stage of life.

As your journey continues, I pray your eyes and ears will be open to see and hear yourself and your children more clearly—the way God sees you. I pray that your God-given senses will be enlightened, that you will truly be "present" in every moment with your kids. Remember, highly trained, intuitive special agents hear, see, feel, and smell important clues that seem unimportant to the untrained agent. In these seemingly unimportant details lay clues to your child's heart. Notice their giggles and their tears, their responses and lack of them, their dancing eyes as well as their disappointment. Smell their mud-stained skin; feel their moppy, messy hair.

I pray that as the seasons change throughout your parenting travels, you will take these treasures and insights and continue to grow closer to God and to your children. If you travel with God, He will be there to meet your need to trust; you can trust Him. He will meet your need to be heard; He will listen. He will support you and give you purpose and value, and He will give you clear direction and boundaries. No matter what season you are in, look up; see God is bigger than what is happening around you. David writes so beautifully in Psalm 32:8, *"I will instruct you and teach you in the way you should go; I will guide you with My eye."* Let Him!

Congratulations, special agent! You have done the work, followed the six clever clues, and made vitally important investigative discoveries. You now have priceless insight and tools to connect to the ever-changing hearts of your children. For that you receive your well-earned badge: *Brave, Honorable, and Courageous Parent.* Wear it proudly!

PART THREE:

LEADER'S GUIDE

Guide for Leading a 13-Week
Small Group

Cracking the Parenting Code:
Guide for Leading a
13-Week Small Group

A lthough *Cracking the Parenting Code* can be read alone or with your spouse, I think there is great benefit in working through it together with other parents. So, congratulations, you are about to embark on an incredible journey. There's no need to be nervous, you are already fully equipped to lead a small group using this book. If you have a desire to see families build strong and loving relationships, you're qualified. As you journey through this book with others, I believe you will experience great fulfillment as you witness the eyes and hearts of parents opening up as they learn to create stronger bonds with their children.

Before You Begin—Wisdom to Make Your Job Easier!

- *People don't care how much you know until they know how much you care.* The most effective groups are groups in which the participants feel that they matter. It's important to convey to them that you genuinely care for them—that you are their biggest cheerleader! You can convey genuine sincerity through good eye contact, body positioning, and listening to what they have to say. When group members feel heard, they feel validated.

- *You don't have to have all the answers to everyone's questions.* That is the beauty of small groups. During discussions, the participants gain deep insight through what others share and what they discover from completing the questions. Don't be afraid of silence; it is in silence that people begin to reflect and, in many cases, gain insight and answers to the questions they have.

- *Validate feelings!* When someone shares a heartfelt insight, it is helpful if you repeat back to them what they shared. They will feel heard. For example: "You felt loved by your father because he had time to listen to you, is that correct?" You don't have to fix their problems. You don't have to come up with an answer. Just repeat what they shared.

- *Be patient as participants share.* Remember it is very difficult to share deep insight into your past and present struggles. Put yourself in the other person's shoes—as they are sharing, they are making themselves vulnerable. Do anything you can to reassure them that what they shared is valuable and enlightening to the group.

- *Stop the gab snatchers!* I've seen it in every group I've been involved in the past 25 years: the person who has a comment about everything. Please don't let one person monopolize your group. Do whatever you can to keep control gracefully. It will make others in the group feel more secure. If you think someone is monopolizing the conversation say, "Thank you so much for sharing your experiences with us. If you don't mind, I'd like to talk with you one-on-one later!" Try to keep the momentum of the group moving and everyone sharing equally.

- *Call on different people to share.* Quiet people have important insights to share, but they often keep their comments to themselves. Your job is to create an opening for them. For instance, you could say, "Paul, I've noticed you nodding. Would you care to elaborate about what you're thinking?" If he says no, don't force the issue, just move on to another person.

Week One: Creating a Bond

Have participants come together in a circle. Begin in prayer. Then ask each person to introduce him or herself and share a little about their life: Married? Divorced? Single? Number of children and their ages? Stepchildren? Foster children? What are their hopes and expectations for this small group? Hand out books. Discuss any scheduling issues or other issues that come up. Each week participants should read the next chapter in *Cracking the Parenting Code* and write down any light-bulb moments they have during the week. End each small group meeting in prayer.

Each week the leader should read (out loud) the following guidelines for the group:

1. *Please don't monopolize the conversation* Women, choose your words carefully. Men, speak up. Often in small groups, women tend to monopolize the conversation. It's very important that no one dominates. If you have a tendency to talk a lot, please try to curb it. If you have a tendency to be quiet, please speak up. It's important that everyone shares.

2. *Please don't interrupt others*

3. *Share only about your own experiences*—not your spouse's, your neighbor's, your children's, or your parent's. There may be some exceptions but this is a good general rule.

4. *Don't tell others how to feel.* Never say, "You shouldn't feel that way." Don't try to fix others' problems. However, if you have had a similar problem and discovered a possible solution, feel free to share it.

5. *What is shared in the group stays within the group*

Weeks 2–12: Learning Together

After praying and reading the guidelines, open each week by sharing a highlight of the chapter, or asking a parent to share. Then give participants the opportunity to comment about what they discovered by answering the FBI Questions from that week's chapter. If the group is more than six people have participants break into groups of two to four for 20 minutes or so to discuss their personal answers. If couples are attending together have them get with one other couple.

After discussing the FBI Questions, call the group together and have an open discussion using the following questions:

Chapter One

1. Are you living your life with the same values and convictions as those your parents raised you with?

2. Are you raising your children similarly to how you were raised?

3. Did you discover anything new about yourself or your children from the questions in this chapter?

4. Do you think it's important for your children to adopt your values and convictions?

5. What are the connections between how you were raised and how you are raising your children?

Chapter Two

1. In Psalm 139 David wrote that God knows every thought, path, word, and wicked way he walked in. He marvels that he cannot flee from God's presence and the way God protects and leads him. What thoughts do the questions in this chapter, associated with Psalm 139, provoke in you?

2. What are the five reasons parents miss what is going on in the hearts of their children?

3. Which of these five obstacles is your greatest challenge and why? (fear, pain, image, effort, denial)

Chapter Three

1. In this chapter we've discovered the importance of searching and understanding our pasts. Why is it important to investigate your past and integrate it into your life story?

2. How do you think your past affects the way you parent?

3. Is it difficult or easy for you to integrate your past into your life story and why?

Chapter Four

1. What does connecting with your children mean to you? Is it a physical, spiritual, or emotional connection?

2. How would any of these connections influence your child's choices?

3. Are you more comfortable relating to your children on a physical, spiritual, or emotional basis?

Chapter Five

1. Do you believe the way parents—married or divorced—treat each other has an impact on their children? How?

2. While reading this chapter, what did you discover about the way you treat your child's other parent?

3. What is the connection between your trustworthiness as a parent and the choices your children will make?

Chapter Six

1. Why was it important for you to be heard when you were a child?

2. What characteristics does a child who has not been heard exhibit? To what and whom would they be drawn? (Friends? Internet? Acting out because of insecurity? Others?)

3. Why do children need to be heard on a consistent basis?

4. Who's going to listen to them if you don't?

Chapter Seven

1. When you answered the questions about where you are investing your time, money, and accomplishments, was there anything that surprised you?

2. How do we teach our children why they are valuable?

3. What behaviors do you see in children who have been taught why they are valuable?

4. Where do you want your children's sense of value to come from?

Chapter Eight

1. How do children develop a sense of purpose?

2. What is the value of teaching our children to serve others?

3. What are the qualities of a child who has been taught and given purpose?

Chapter Nine

1. How do you think your experiences as a child affect the way you support your children?

2. Why is it important for us as parents to know the specific ways in which our children need to be supported?

3. In what ways do your children need your support?

4. When would you choose to allow your children more independence in order to support them?

Chapter Ten

1. What boundaries and limits do you believe children consistently need?

2. Is it important that you and your child's other parent enforce the same boundaries, limits, and rules for your children?

3. How do you know if a boundary is too lenient or too strict?

Chapter Eleven

1. In this chapter you've read how children and parents go through seasons. Can you identify your current season?

- Summer—children are warm and snuggly

- Fall—children are snuggly one day, claws the next

- Winter—children are distant eventually breaking away

- Spring—children are hopeful; you are hopeful

2. Do you find it difficult to surrender your children to God?

3. What is the most powerful discovery you've made in this investigation?

Week 13: Celebrate
Special agent graduation! Get creative, have a party!

Acknowledgments

How God brought this book together is nothing short of a miracle. I had been researching and teaching workshops on these parenting principles for several months, and the burden was great. I felt a nudge to write what I was learning. There was one problem; I didn't know how to write. Besides, I didn't think I had the discipline, and I had no idea were to start. I asked others to write it for me—doors were slammed, windows were shut.

When I was about to give up, my husband and I visited a new church in Arizona, where we were living at the time. As we walked in the door, we were greeted by Alice Gray. I was shocked. She is an accomplished writer *(Stories for the Heart)*. Thank you, Alice, because from that God-ordained minute, you steered me in the right direction, took time away from your own writing deadlines, and dropped nuggets of wisdom and insight into my hands. I think I'm going to change your name from Alice Gray to Alice Gracious!

Throughout the life-changing twists and investigative turns in this book, I experienced incredible highs and devastating lows. On the most difficult days, I truly felt like a failure, and it was crippling. I couldn't get out of bed, so I stayed there, with my Bible, my computer, and God.

"I can't do this," I'd whine.

I'd hear His gentle voice, "I know. But I can. Let Me." And He did. He met me and He brought pivotal people at pivotal times who encouraged, guided, and directed me.

My husband, my boyfriend, and my best friend, Randy— I am so glad you're all those rolled into one person. Since the day we met, you have made me feel like the prettiest, funniest gal on planet Earth. You have laughed and cried with me through almost 27 years of parenting. You have believed in me, even on dark days when I didn't believe in myself. Thank you for not letting me give up.

My mama, you have always been my ultimate encourager. Thank you for showing me what unconditional love looks and feels like. You truly are a woman of dignity and perseverance. I love you.

My stepdad, Jack Witherite: we started out shaky (to say the least), and have grown to love one another, which truly is a testimony to God.

Heidi Lee, my firstborn, my daughter. God has used you to mold me into the person I am today. It delights my heart to see the way you interact with and are training your children. I pray that you know how much I love you and that I am truly sorry for my many failures as a parent.

Nicholas, my son. Thanks for keeping me laughing and on my toes. "Mom, you really know how much I hate to read, but I really want to read this book. I want to see what made you start listening to me in these last six months."

Susie Behrman, who prayed, listened, and processed, then encouraged and challenged me every step of the way to take the high road. This book wouldn't be what it is today if you hadn't lent me your "elephant ears" while biking along the Willamette River; helped me process important discoveries I made in my own life, while sipping tea in your log cabin and countless restaurants; and spent thousands of hours praying for our children as well as each other, hiking the trail for more than 26 years in Beavercreek. I am proud to call you my friend.

Ryan Mathew Goddard, my son-in-law. It thrills my heart to see how much you delight in God, in my daughter, and in my grandchildren. Did you know you delight my heart?

My gentle-spirited daughter-in-law, Tiffany, who has wisdom beyond her years and has lovingly allowed me to be a part of her life.

My seven little dwarfs, my seven little darlings (soon to be eight): Joshua Randale, Trinity Diane, Rachel Laura, Nathaniel Ryan, Isaiah Laurin, Leah Grace, and Amanda Joy. Though you each are still very small, you bring huge bursts of radiant joy into my life. When I see you little tornadoes barreling toward me screaming, "Grandma, Grandma," I feel as though I have died and gone to heaven, with seven precious angels twirling around me. I am the most blessed person on the face of the earth because you call me Grandma!

My sisters, Cheri Rizzo and Diane Grina, and my brother, Randy Grina, who together taught me to sing harmony on those twisty Carver curves. Guys, Grandma Grina left so many of her incredibly fun-loving qualities in all of you. I thank God that her legacy lives on in us! Cheri, how precious was the day you took me skiing on Mt. Hood in my darkest hour, and then we came down off the mountain to the acceptance letter from New Hope Publishers. What a glorious day!

My other parents: Laurin and Ruby Heinsohn, you've been so wonderfully supportive of me.

My prayer partners, Jennifer Evans, Andrea Springer, Becky Mitchell, Leslie White, and Jo Marie Garibaldi for lifting me up to God and sharing my tears.

Annie Bernard, Cindy and Maureen Rotter, and Greg Rice, Amee Spadaro, and Rachel Ravan for your honesty and insight about your childhoods and parenting.

Linda Whitmore-Stevenson, Pam Ravan, Caroline Whitmore Brandy Lewis, Michelle Rizzo, Cheyloa and Anthony Chase, Jana and Scott Matthews, Karen Wilkinson, Paula Harbaugh. Joanna Forrester, Shelly Pendergrass, Jo Marie Garibaldi, Darla and Glen Harman, Katie Harman, Tom and Laura Sparks, Mindy and Aaron Murdock, Peggy Roloff.

The Gathering Girls: Linda Smith, Sara Jossi, Debbie Birch, Carol Charnstrom, Mokihana White, Linda Shaddy, Julie Garren, Diane Davidson, Akemi McKee, Connie Miller, Lindy Batdorf, Dee Bedsole.

My creative consultant and friend, Kerry Hubbard.

The Bee-Bop Kids: You know who you are!

My Brazilian Kids: *Obrigado!*

My "uther muther" kids: Molly and Susanne Behrman—thank you for sharing your mother with me.

Bev Tharan and the girls at Teen Challenge Home of Hope in Casa Grande, Arizona.

My pastors Jerry and Joan Sanford, Rich and Debbie Palmer, and Gary and Charlene Poston: thank you for teaching me the Word of God, living a life that glorifies Him, and believing in the FBI Parent ministry.

Thank you, Doreen Button, for believing in the message of this book and painstakingly editing this project for over three years. I thank you for not giving up, and for your brutal honesty. Even though we've only met in cyberspace, God has used you. The day you emailed me and wisely said, "I am so sorry for all the pain you're going through. But your writing is much deeper, much richer." You gave me hope!

Thank you, Gloria, my writing coach, for not laughing in my face the first time you read what I had written. Thanks for coaching me in the right direction.

Tammy Dunahoo for spiritual insight; professional counselor Paula Lupo for your support and encouragement; Investigator Joanne Zylstra and Sergeant Dean Hennessey for helping me understand the insightful world of investigating.

Rick Brown who led me so graciously to the loving arms of God.

I want to thank the hundreds of you from all over the United States, Europe, Australia, and Brazil who bravely and courageously let me into your lives, sharing your vulnerable hearts and tears in hopes that your experiences and insights will help others.

My new friends at New Hope Publishers: Andrea Mullins, Randy Bishop, Jonathan Howe, Ashley Crafton, and staff. Thank you for your patience with this green writer.

To my beloved Jesus, as I've searched for endless clues, You have guided and encouraged me to go deeper, to find hidden treasures. I discovered the ultimate treasure: many magnificent undiscovered facets of You! Your gentle grace and tender mercy carried me; Your unconditional love continually comforted me;

Your powerful words sustained me. I am eternally grateful. I give these words to You. They are a testimony to all You have done in my life! I thank You that I have this treasure in my earthen vessel, that the excellence of the power is Yours not mine. (See 2 Corinthians 4:7.) I love You.

Author's Recommended Resources

Dads Connecting with Daughters
She Calls Me Daddy: Seven Things Every Man Needs to Know About Building a Complete Daughter, Robert Wolgemuth
Daughters Gone Wild, Dads Gone Crazy: Battle-Tested Tips From a Father and Daughter Who Survived the Teenage Years, Charles Stone, Heather Stone

Dads Connecting with Sons
Raising a Modern-Day Knight: A Father's Role in Guiding His Son to Authentic Manhood, Robert Lewis
It's Better to Build Boys than Mend Men, S. Truett Cathy, founder of Chick-Fil-A

Moms Connecting with Teen Daughters
Mom, I Hate My Life!: Becoming Your Daughter's Ally Through the Emotional Ups and Downs of Adolescence, Sharon A. Hersh
Mom, I Feel Fat!: Becoming Your Daughter's Ally in Developing a Healthy Body Image, Sharon A. Hersh
"I'm Not Mad, I Just Hate You!": A New Understanding of Mother-Daughter Conflict, Roni Cohen-Sandler and Michelle Silver

Moms Connecting with Sons
That's My Son: How Moms Can Influence Boys to Become Men of Character, Rick Johnson
Making Sense of the Men in Your Life, Kevin Leman

Connecting with Stepchildren
Winning the Heart of Your Stepchild, Robert G. Barnes
7 Steps to Bonding with Your Stepchild, Suzen J. Ziegahn

Single Parenting

Single Parenting that Works, Kevin Leman

What Children Need to Know When Parents Get Divorced, William L. Coleman

The Single Dad's Survival Guide: How to Succeed as a One-Man Parenting Team, Mike Klumpp

101 Ways to Be a Long-Distance Super-Dad…or Mom Too!, George Newman

Healing from a Bad Childhood

A Dad-Shaped Hole in My Heart: How God Wants to Heal the Wounds Left by Your Earthly Father, H. Norman Wright

Boundaries, Trust, and Value

Parenting with Love and Logic: Teaching Children Responsibility, Foster Cline, MD and Jim Fay

Boundaries with Kids: When to Say Yes, When to Say No, to Help Your Children Gain Control of Their Lives, Dr. Henry Cloud and Dr. John Townsend

The New Strong-Willed Child, Dr. James Dobson

Purpose and Support

Wired by God: Empowering Your Teen for a Life of Passion and Purpose, Joe White with Larry Weeden

Raising Kids Who Will Make a Difference: Helping Your Family Live with Integrity, Value Simplicity, and Care for Others, Susan V. Vogt

Setting Up Stones: A Parent's Guide to Making Your Home a Place of Worship, Martha and Greg Singleton

Missions Moments 2: 52 Easy-to-Use Missional Messages and Activities for Today's Family, Mitzi Eaker

Ministry Opportunities:

www.worldventure.com

www.teenmania.com

www.wmu.com/VolunteerConnection

Sponsoring an Orphan:
www.childcareworldwide.org

Listening
How to Talk So Your Kids Will Listen, from Toddlers to Teenagers: Connecting with Your Children at Every Age, H. Norman Wright

Seminars
Love and Logic Seminars
Cline/Fay Institute, Inc.
www.loveandlogic.com
1-800-338-4065

Five Love Languages
www.garychapman.org

The National Institute of Marriage
www.nationalmarriage.com
(417) 335-5882

FBI Parenting Workshops
www.fbiparent.com
www.lauraleeheinsohn.com

Web Sites
Focus on the Family
www.family.org

New Hope® Publishers is a division of WMU®,
an international organization that challenges Christian
believers to understand and be radically involved in God's
mission. For more information about WMU,
go to www.wmu.com. More information about
New Hope books may be found at
www.newhopepublishers.com. New Hope books may
be purchased at your local bookstore.

MORE PARENTING RESOURCES
from New Hope

Missions Moments 2
*52 Easy-to-Use Missional Messages
and Activities for Today's Family*
Mitzi Eaker
978-1-59669-210-7
N087101 • $12.99

Setting Up Stones
*A Parent's Guide to Making Your Home
a Place of Worship*
Martha and Greg Singleton
978-1-59669-219-0
N084142 • $12.99

Coach Mom
*7 Strategies for Organizing
Your Family into an All-Star Team*
Brenna Stull
978-1-59669-022-6
N074125 • $14.99

Love Notes in Lunchboxes
*And Other Ideas to
Color Your Child's Day*
Linda J. Gilden
978-1-56309-821-5
N044109 • $9.99

Available in bookstores everywhere

For information about these books or
any New Hope product, visit www.newhopepublishers.com.